Ho

Like a Book

A Guide to Speed-Reading People, Understand Body Language and Emotions, Decode Intentions, and Connect Effortlessly

losses, direct or indirect, which are incurred as a result of the use of information contained within this document, including, but not limited to, — errors, omissions, or inaccuracies.

Table of Contents

2 FREE Gifts

To help you along your personal growth journey, I've created 2 FREE bonus books that will help you master your mind, become more confident, and eliminate intrusive thoughts.

You can get instant access by signing up to my email newsletter below.

On top of the 2 free books, you will also receive weekly tips along with free book giveaways, discounts, and more.

All of these bonuses are 100% free with no strings attached. You don't need to provide any personal information except your email address.

To get your bonus, go to:

https://theartofmastery.com/confidence/

Free Bonus Book #1: *Master Your Mind: 11 Mental Hacks to Eliminate Negative Thoughts, Improve Your Emotional Intelligence, and End Procrastination*

Discover the techniques and strategies backed by scientific and psychological studies that dive into why your mind is preventing you from achieving success in life and how to fix them.

You will learn how to:

- Deal with stress, fear, and anxiety
- Become more emotionally intelligent
- Communicate better in your relationships
- Overcome any and all limiting beliefs you have
- Avoid procrastinating
- Actually enjoy doing difficult tasks
- And so much more!

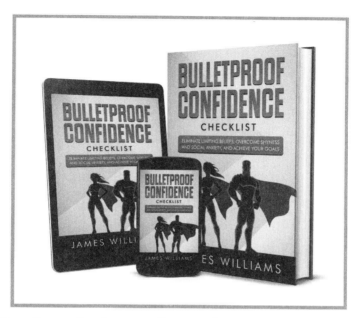

<u>Free Bonus Book #2</u>: *Bulletproof Confidence Checklist: Eliminate Limiting Beliefs, Overcome Shyness and Social Anxiety, and Achieve Your Goals*

In this book you will discover how to overcome the limiting beliefs that results in lack of confidence and social anxiety.

You will learn practical tips to rewire your negative thought patterns, break free from shyness, and become the best version of yourself.

Introduction

First things first, I'd like to start by saying thank you for purchasing this book. As the title confesses, this book is all about learning how to read people like, well, a book, in order to communicate effectively, nurture meaningful relationships, and ultimately connect with others effortlessly. I can't stress this latter part enough—I want this book to help you CONNECT with people, forge relationships, and for the most part strengthen your existing ties with others around you.

As you've probably heard a million times before, communication is everything when it comes to relationships, and if you're able to master the art of just that, then your relationships have the opportunity to benefit endlessly.

But we'll get to how to develop these skills in time. Let's start at the beginning. My name's James. It's nice to meet you. I've been studying body language and verbal communication for a very long time. Amazing how quickly the years go! I got my start from my interest in TV shows that seemed to glamorize body language and profiling. This started with your traditional crime and thriller TV shows that would profile in the very literal sense, but this evolved over time. When I began to look into commercials and advertisers and the way people are presenting themselves, the over-sexualization of modern reality TV shows, and more recently, social media influencing and other forms of online content I couldn't help but find it all fascinating. However, and perhaps most importantly, I was interested in learning about verbal communication and effective communication in general because I wasn't happy with the way I was living life.

I used to live life suffering from severe shyness and social anxiety, which basically crippled me in almost any social interaction. Upon taking the time to learn how to compose myself and connect with others, using some of the strategies you're about to learn in the following chapters, I also naturally learned how to see what I was learning in others, aka, reading them. I then dedicated my time to learning this art of how to *read people* and how it would help me connect with them easier.

While the television shows and movies make reading people seem like a fine art, in reality, there's really nothing glamorous about it. The process of reading other people is instead grounded on cold-hard science and research. I'm grateful for this opportunity to share what I know with you and this journey I've been on over the last decade or so—especially since it helped me so much in life and can do the same in yours! Learning to read between the lines allowed me to advance in my career, marry the woman of my dreams, nurture a good relationship with my kids, and become so fulfilled in many of my social circles. Even talking to strangers, something I would never have even dreamed of years ago, has become such a satisfying experience because of these skills.

Knowing how to communicate properly with people is the hallmark of good relationships. These methods that you're about to learn have given me the kind of deep relationships that I could only dream about before.

However, all these ideas of amazing communication start to beg the questions of how did it get so bad in the first place?

How did we get to this point in our lives? Why do we find it so hard to connect and communicate with people?

There are plenty of answers. One of the most popular is that many people don't always say what they mean or even what they want to say. Whether they're hiding the truth or conforming because they're trying to send a good impression doesn't matter. It's this style of communication that leads to mixed signals, confusion, and everyone ends up getting something out of an interaction that they really didn't want to get.

Let's look at a real-world view. Have you ever given a presentation and noticed people dozing off or not paying attention? Have you ever had problems with your boss for reasons that you just can't grasp? Perhaps your manager quickly latches on to suggestions made by a coworker when you suggested the exact same thing before?

Or look at your dating life. Do you always strike out with your dates? Do you find yourself unsure of what to do or what to say when spending time with someone? Do you have a hard time figuring out whether the other person is actually into you?

Even in your family life, do you find your partner is dismissive, or do your conversations always end in arguments? Do you find your relationship boring, or do you have an unshakable feeling of disconnect, regardless of how mild it may feel, from those you share your life with?

These are all problems that can be solved with just the right amount of insight when it comes to body language. Body language will tell you at what point your boss has lost interest or which part of the presentation is perceived as boring by your office mates, enabling you to bring the conversation back around by recapturing their attention in just the right way.

These skills can also tell you when a date is interested in having the date even before you walk towards them in a bar. These skills will help you listen more thoroughly, will help you easily identify great conversation subjects, and will help you guide your conversations in an It will also show you how to be more confident in both situations or, at least, cause others to perceive you in this way.

Knowing how to master this art gives you the chance to assess and change direction through any interaction as needed. This knowledge can help you formulate your techniques depending on what the audience needs and what you want to achieve. Simply put, it can help you fulfill goals through subtle but effective means.

This isn't pseudo-science either. Studies have shown that body language has a huge impact on day-to-day conversations. A large part of human communication is done through body language.

The good news is that you don't have to spend thousands of dollars on classes to learn these techniques. This book can help you with those and so much more! Throughout the following chapters, I intend to help you learn how to figure out the different personality types you'll come across in your day-to-day life and the unique traits each one has, communicate with these different personality types, how to read body language in any situation, how to understand verbal cues, and of course—how to train yourself to become a better reader of the people around you.

I want you to be able to achieve bigger and better things through this book, so don't wait around—flip over to the next page and let's begin!

Chapter 1: The Science Behind Reading People and Who They Are

The way in which people think, what they think about, or why they do what they do has created an entire branch of science called *Personality Psychology*. It's basically a branch of psychology that studies personality, no surprises there, and how they differ from one person to the next.

The study deals with the construction of a coherent picture of an individual, their psychological process, psychological differences, psychological similarities, and human nature. Don't worry if that sounds a little complicated. It basically is a science that helps us comprehensively describe how people are and aims to figure out why.

To really break it down, the science tries to answer these five questions:

- What traits make up a person?
- How does a person think?
- What makes one personality different from another?
- What makes one personality similar to another?

- What personality traits are already present from the moment a person is born?

It seems like such a simple five-question study at first, but it's really such a massive field that I doubt any book will be able to discuss everything about people without being incredibly long-winded. Nevertheless, we will take the teachings from this study and apply them to our own practices of reading people and enhancing our abilities to communicate.

With this science under your belt, you'll be able to develop a hard understanding of why people act and think the way they do, which will directly impact how you interrupt their verbal and non-verbal communication. This comes together enabling you to read people accurately.

What Is Personality?

Personality has many definitions, but for this book, we're going to define it as a set of characteristics possessed by an individual.

This set of characteristics influences a person's cognition, emotion, motivation, behavior, and the way they interact with their environment. This is why people act differently around different people and in different places. Some even call this 'the mask that we wear', and people will wear different masks at different points in their lives.

In fact, the word *personality* originated from the Latin word *persona*, which means *mask*.

Studies targeted towards defining, describing, and categorizing personality have been around years. The ever-popular Zodiac signs are actually a way to categorize personality based on a birthdate. Of course, since this way of categorizing personality isn't backed by science, we won't be talking about it, but it does go to show that this line of identifying people is nothing new.

Instead, we shall be focusing on the facts backed by lots of juicy studies, starting with one of the most common ways of defining people.

Introvert and Extrovert

Two personality types you've certainly heard before, and one you probably have a very good idea of which you are. The common belief is that introverts are quiet, and extroverts are loud. However, this is just a basic meaning that's just a manifestation of what makes each personality unique. The main difference between an extrovert and an introvert is how their brains operate. That's right—this goes all the way to the brain, and scientific studies prove it.

Studies show that an extrovert's dopamine trigger is typically shorter than that of an introvert. Dopamine is the body's happy hormone, and accordingly, stimulation for extroverts runs the path of taste, touch, visual, and auditory sensory processing. It's quick and very much felt by all five senses. This is why when extroverts gamble, the rush they get is stronger and faster. Introverts, on the other hand, run a more complicated course. The dopamine pathway runs through planning, remembering, and solving problems.

What does this all mean? Extroverts have a brain makeup that encourages them to seek fast-rewards, while the same does not hold true for introverts. In other words, an extrovert gets their high from hard and fast sources of stimulation. An introvert likes slow and steady. This is why extroverts seem more in your face and more eager to get into new experiences than introverts.

This difference between the two types will tell you how you want to communicate or enable a connection with another person. For example, if you're planning a birthday party for an introvert, a small quiet event would be closer to their style.

In the context of this book, when you're having a conversation with an introvert, you'll want to prioritize your approach to be cool, calm, and collected, whereas when you're chatting with an extrovert, you'll want to try and match their energy to connect with them in the best possible way.

And with that, you've just read someone and acted accordingly! Nice. I suppose you can read people now, so we'll just end here. I joke, of course. This is but one way you can read people. However, it's no lie that making a small change like this in the way you communicate will bring about massive benefits in the way you connect with others.

Myers Briggs Type Indicator

An online search for a term like *personalities* or *how to identify someone's personality* will bring up dozens or even hundreds of pages dedicated to the Myers Briggs Type Indicator, also known as the MBTI Personality Test. This test was popularized by Carl Jung and was commonly once used by companies for hiring purposes. Carl Jung was the main proponent of this personality identification and was the psychoanalyst and psychiatrist who founded analytical psychology.

Under the MBTI personality characterization, the introvert and extrovert classifications have been expanded. Instead of the traditional introvert versus extrovert, personalities are now typed depending on eight different categories.

Under the MBTI school of thought, you can either be:

- Introverted or Extroverted
- Sensing or INtuitive
- Thinking or Feeling
- Perceiving or Judging

The IN in intuitive is intentional. I'll explain in a second, although you may already be familiar with it yourself if you've completed a test like this. Lots of people like to do this test for fun since the results can be scarily accurate. If you want to try it for yourself, I highly recommend trying the *16 Personalities* test, which can be found with a quick online search. Complete this test, and it will tell you your personality type and describe what kind of person you are, how you think, how you perceive the world, and so on.

In total, there are 16 Personality Types under the MBTI principle, which are formed from a combination of the eight categories listed above. So, how does this work?

Let's say the test concludes you're an Introvert, an INtuitive, a Thinker, and Judging, so your personality type is: INTJ.

On the flip side, you could be an Extrovert, an Intuitive, a Sensor, and a Perceiver—making you an ENSP. All possible combinations of these characteristics create 16 different personalities, and each one has its own unique charm and, of course, its own unique vice. What I want you to understand, however, is that ESFP is not the automatic opposite of INTJ just because all the letters are flipped. It's far more complicated than that, which is why it can be tough to fully explain. For clarity, just treat every category as its own separate identity.

What do the letters mean?

So, now you understand how these personality types are defined, let's break down what they actually mean. Let's cut straight to the chase.

Personality Type	Definition
Extraversion	These are people who tend to focus on and have interest in people and experiences outside of themselves and from external elements.
Introversion	These are people who tend to naturally look within themselves for interest, having a focus on their ideas, feelings, and inner impressions.
Sensing	Sensing people like to look at the present moment when making decisions and will use as much concrete information as possible before deciding what to do next.
iNtuition	Intuitive people much prefer to focus on the outcomes of events and look for possible patterns and possibilities in any given situation.
Thinking	People who tend to think more about their decisions and will apply logic to their process. These people also tend

	to be more analytical than others and will think about the cause and effect of various situations.
Feeling	This group of people are more tuned into their feelings and emotions and tend to rely on their gut instinct more than anything else. They will usually take the person-orientated approach to a situation.
Judgment	These are people who much prefer to be planned and organized in their life and are most comfortable when things are laid out before them in clear, actionable ways.
Perception	These people are more likely to be flexible and spontaneous in any given situation. They don't need scheduling or a plan to feel comfortable and are very much the kinds of people to go with the flow.

Using these personality types alone, you should already start to see how both you and the people in your life start to come together and fit into these categories. I'm going to talk more about how you can integrate these identifications into how you read people later.

However, for now I just want you to start trying to read people you encounter in your life and see which of these terms describe them. Already, you should start to see how you act back and communicate with these people that will create better interactions instantaneously.

Now, it's important to add that you're not going to be able to judge people based on their personality types. It's unlikely you'll be able to convince your boss to take this test just so you can know how to interact and communicate with them. This might be possible with your partner or kids because it can be a fun little exercise, but it won't be possible all the time.

What you need to know is to write down notes that will help you remember the personality types out there. Maybe you want to take your boss and write down some of the traits they're shared throughout your experience with them. For example, are they the sort of person to be strictly scheduled, or do they like to go with the flow?

Having the kind of mindset where you're on the lookout for these kinds of personality traits will put you on the right path to reading people properly.

Enneagram Personality Typing

While you should cover most bases with the Myers Briggs personality test, you may like to try the Enneagram of Personality school of thought, where you'll find there are a total of nine different personality types. While this isn't essential, I find it all very interesting and if you find these personality types easier to remember and manage, then I highly recommend using them instead. Remember, it's all about figuring out what works for you.

All the Enneagram personality types are interconnected and were principally derived from the teachings of a Chilean psychiatrist, Claudio Naranjo. Like the MBTI identifications, the Enneagram was also used in business management to help business owners gain insight into their employees and their fitness for specific roles. Nowadays, it's not considered a huge determining factor for hiring, but some companies may still use it to guide their hiring process.

Here's a quick look at the different personality types as defined under the Enneagram System.

Personality Types	Description
The Reformer	Rational, principled, purposeful, perfectionist, self-controlled, and idealistic
The Helper	Caring, demonstrative, generous, possessive, people-pleasing, and interpersonal

The Achiever	Success-oriented, adaptive, excelling, image-conscious, driven, and pragmatic
The Individualist	Sensitive, expressive, dramatic, temperamental, self-absorbed, and withdrawn
The Investigator	The cerebral type, perceptive, secretive, isolated, innovative, and intense
The Loyalist	Committed, engaging, anxious, suspicious, responsible, and security-oriented
The Enthusiast	Busy, fun-loving, versatile, scattered, distractible, and spontaneous
The Challenger	Dominating, decisive, confrontational, self-confident, willful, and powerful
The Peacemaker	Easygoing, receptive, reassuring, complacent, agreeable, and self-effacing

Of course, this is just an outline of personality types you could use, but just like the Myers Briggs setup, it's all about guiding your mind in such a way that you're looking at the people you're communicating with and come across in your life and defining what kind of person they are.

It's when you can do this that you'll be able to read between the lines of what they're saying and what they mean, can find out the truth to their words, and figure out what they're actually thinking.

Reread them and submit them to memory. It doesn't have to be word for word, just a general idea of the types and what you're looking out for.

When you meet someone, or you're interacting with someone, bear these traits in mind. For example, say you speak to your boss all the time, but you've never really taken the time to define them using a category system such as this.

If you're looking to actively improve your communication with them, start thinking about what characteristics describe them. It might even help to write some sort of personal statement about them and the type of person they are. You might write something like:

My boss likes to get things done. He always has a plan and is always looking for ways to improve existing ways of working. He is very confident in his abilities, likes to lay down the law, and runs a tight ship. He is decisive and quick to make a decision.

Even from this short statement, you could identify your boss as a Challenger type personality, which means that talking to him about feelings and emotions is not usually going to get a good response. However, if you approach him with hard, actionable data, he's very much going to be on your side.

You now know that they prefer to talk about the details of a project and get straight to planning and organizing everything. They never really just go with the flow or hope things will turn out okay.

With this information by your side, you can now start communicating effectively with your boss far more precisely than you have before, and in a way that they'll really connect with. The more they resonate with you, the better the results of your interactions will be, and the ceiling for which your relationship can grow becomes limitless.

If you haven't already, I highly recommend taking the test yourself or have a read through the personality types and you'll be able to start applying them to people in your life.

The Spectrum of All Personality Types

I can't stress this enough—personality is a spectrum meaning there's no set or permanent personality type. A person isn't 100% introvert or extrovert. This designation is merely a *preference*. To make matters more complex, people can even change throughout their lives, but usually not too much.

You can use this information to try to identify the kinds of people in your life and alter your interactions accordingly. We're going to talk about how to do all this in a later chapter, but for now, let's continue our journey into the art of reading people.

Chapter 2: An Introduction to Reading Body Language

So, at this point, you have some ideas what to think about when heading into a conversation with anyone, and the ideas you've learned around are ideal when trying to figure out how to communicate with someone while trying to engage with what they're saying. However, and this is a big however, it doesn't really help you *read* the person you're talking with in the present moment.

As I said before, personalities tend to sit on a spectrum, so you're going to need skills that will help you read the body language, the expressions, and really take onboard the words that someone is saying to you while recognizing the inflection in which they're saying it.

I want to say this right now, these aren't skills reserved for the extroverted and most charismatic humans amongst us. Far from it. Like everything in life, of course there are people who are naturally talented at reading people, but it is very much a skill that can be learned and practiced once you know what you're doing and what you're looking for.

Once you gain an understanding of the strategies and techniques we'll explore from here on out, it's up to you to put them into practice. You're not going to get it right every time, nor will it be super easy at first. However, the more you practice these techniques, the more confident you'll become and the better, more accurate your results will be.

It all starts here with building up your understanding of what to look out for, so let's start with the basics. An introduction to reading body language, including what it is, what the benefits are, and some of the obstacles you may experience along the way. If you can learn all this now, then you won't need to figure it out the hard way!

That's what this chapter is all about. We're going to explore the advantages and pitfalls of reading body language. The fact is that body language is an inexact science, and as much as it can be useful, there will also be some hardships you'll need to become aware of.

The Impact of Culture

One thing I want you to consider is the impact of culture on body language.

When trying to communicate with people, whether verbally or nonverbally, you will find that there are certain actions unique to certain cultures that are different in other parts of the world.

A really clear example of this comes from Asian countries where bowing is a sincere sign of respect. However, in American and other Western countries, the typical *bow* has been shortened to a simple nod of the head to someone. Also note that in Asian countries, the depth of the bow indicates the depth of respect one

25

might have for the other person. This just doesn't tend to happen in the Western world whatsoever.

Why is this problematic? Well, if you're trying to communicate with someone of a different background, you will have to do your research on their culture. What gestures are considered proper, and which ones are a show of respect? While the other person may understand that you're from a different background and don't know about their gestures, you will find that making that extra effort can make you stand out from the crowd, which will do wonders for how other people perceive and treat you.

This is an incredibly interesting point and can vary with severity.

If you're going on vacation to a country with a different culture, people will see you and most will assume that you won't know the traditions. However, taking the time to learn and practice, and ultimately applying them when you're in the country, will garner so much respect, and it may open new opportunities that you wouldn't have had access to before.

This applies to the entire art of reading people. It requires you to put in time and effort. Whether you're reading people for work, preparing for a meeting with a client who lives on the other side of the world, or just practicing by talking to people outside your social circles, experience is your best friend.

And you can only get experience if you're willing to put the work in. For some ideas to get you started, here are some cultural differences to keep your eyes open for.

Gesture	Meaning
Nodding	For Americans, nodding to someone speaking signifies you agree with what they're saying or that you're paying attention to what they're saying. However, in Bulgaria and Greece, this gesture indicates that you disagree with what they say.
Giving the Middle Finger	We could flip the bird if we wanted to upset someone in the United States. One of the most disrespectful expressions in our culture is the middle finger. But don't be offended if you find yourself in China's sea of middle fingers—it's the finger people use to point with and doesn't indicate malice.
Keeping Your Hands Below	Children in the United States are taught not to eat with their arms on

the Dinner Table	the table.
	However, it is customary in France to keep your hands on the table, palms down, on either side of your dish.
	Your host will wonder what you're doing with your hands if they slide below the table.
Crossing Your Arms	Crossed arms may be a subtle sign of meanness or wrath in America, but it's how many individuals rest their arms reflexively.
	In Finland, though, it's advisable to avoid using this gesture totally because it could indicate that you're causing trouble or beginning a battle.
Waving Goodbye	Waving goodbye is ingrained in the American psyche as a way of saying goodbye and is a simple gesture unlikely to upset anyone.
	However, this gesture is used to say "no" rather than "goodbye" in parts

	of Europe and South America.
Generally Using Your Left Hand	People in some parts of the United States still have trouble using their left hand, while the left hand is still associated with personal hygiene in large parts of Africa, Asia, and the Middle East. Touching someone or using something with your left hand, which is typically used for toilet paper, is a no-no. It's also not a good idea to shake hands.
Placing Your Hands Together in a Prayer Stance	When praying in the United States, people often place their palms near their chests. Nepal, on the other hand, is a traditional and friendly way of greeting or saying farewell to someone.
The Peace Sign (V-	Originally, the letter "v" stood for "victory."

Fingers)	It is now known as the "peace symbol."
	It's noticeable when individuals are attempting to evoke hippies, and it's such an iconic element of photography in Japanese society that Time Magazine wrote an article on where it came from.
	As a result, please make sure your palm is facing away from you.
	Since at least 1330, this symbol (with the palm facing inward) has had the same meaning as the middle finger in Australia and the United Kingdom.
	You'll be shouting "F*** You!" in those countries, which appears to be the polar opposite of "peace."
To Point at	For a long time, pointing towards

Someone	someone in the United States was regarded as a semi-aggressive action, but it has now evolved into a hilarious symbol of acceptance.
	This gesture, however, is deemed highly offensive in many countries around the world.
	In several African countries, pointing at things rather than people is acceptable.
Two Thumbs Up	In the United States, this usually translates to "Wonderful job!"
	It signifies "Up yours!" in Greece, Latin America, the Middle East, Russia, and other places.
Finger and Thumb Together (A-Okay)	In the United States, making a circle with your thumb and pointer finger usually denotes "OK!"
	It depicts the evil eye in some Middle Eastern countries.
	"You're an a**hole, according to a more popular definition."
	This is how Greece, Spain, and Brazil interpret it.
	Turkey's gesture has a second level

	of homophobic connotation.
	Nixon is famous for making this first impression on a country.
	That is something you should never do.
	In the United States, white nationalists have recently co-opted the sign for their own goals, altering the seemingly innocuous original meaning depending on the situation.
Crossing Your Fingers	It's a rather generic method of invoking good luck to an American.
	Women in tone-deaf romantic comedies are the only ones who do it, yet the concept is nonetheless acknowledged.
	In Vietnam, however, the gesture is thought to be... clearly feminine.
	Consider it a female version of yelling at someone.
Imitating Animals Horns on Your Head	Although this symbol isn't very well-known in the United States, we may use it to imitate a horned animal or to be amusing.
	In Japan, though, it is not such a

| | witty sign. |
| | Instead, this motion resembles devil horns, implying that someone is really unhappy. |

It's Possible to Rely Too Much on Body Language

While body language is such an essential part of communication, I must note that body language is still supplemental to actually listening and won't also give you the full story.

Basically, reading someone's body language isn't the be-all and end-all when it comes to hearing what someone is saying, just like only listening to what they're saying isn't. You need to combine both listening and reading someone to acquire the full and honest picture of what they're saying and can't just rely on one technique.

Think of it this way. Imagine you're looking into a room, and you see two people talking. There's a thick pane of glass between you and the other people so you can't hear what's being said, but you can see everything crystal clearly. You see one person shaking their head vigorously. What are they saying?

- No, they don't agree with what is being said.
- They cannot believe what is being said

- They are imitating someone else who is saying no

- They don't want to believe what they are hearing

- They are so happy they can't believe what is happening

- They are so sad they can't believe what is happening

As you can see, what message the body language is sending relies directly on the context of the conversation in which it's happening, so you need to be paying attention, and not making any assumptions.

Body language will give you an insight into what a person thinks or feels inside, but you also shouldn't ignore what they're saying. Listen to what they're telling you first and if you're confused or unsure, look at their body language.

This should more or less tell you about the lay of the land. Remember, there are instances when listening is better than simply watching a person's body language. The fact is that in many cases, body language is simply used to emphasize what they're already saying, so it's best if you listen AND look.

The Power of Groups

Being part of a group is another obstacle when trying to read people's thoughts, ideas, expressions, and body language. Groups tend to affect how a person approaches a particular situation, especially when put under pressure. I'm sure that at some point in your life you changed your mind because of the pressures that come from being in a group.

They might be all in agreement over a particular course of action, and you feel forced to agree with that decision. Or perhaps you've made a decision in order to look good in that particular group. Conformity is the magic word when it comes to groups. Every person wants to be accepted by the community, and in order to do so, they have to *conform* to what the community thinks must be done.

This is why it can be tough to spot an introvert during a party because some introverts conform to extrovert characteristics when thrown into the company of extroverts. In fact, a study was conducted to measure just how badly a group can affect a person's decision.

When made to choose between what they believe to be the *right* answer and what the group thinks, 75% of people chose the group answer, despite the fact that it was the wrong one.

One of my favorite examples of this was on the UK television show featuring psychological illusionist Derren Brown. He set up a room where he was auditioning people for a role. There was a line of ten chairs for those who were auditioning to fill out forms while waiting to be called. The first two seats were filled with actors.

Members of the public came in and sat next to the actors. In the room, a bell sound was played, and the actors stood up, doing nothing else but continuing to write on their form as though standing up to a bell was completely normal. The members of the public were not told to do this.

As the set went on and the actors stood up and sat back down with each bell played, some members of the public would join in with the standing and sitting, despite never being told to do anything. They were simply conforming because they didn't want to be left out of the group, despite there being no obligation to do anything.

In some cases, groups can be so powerful that they can *normalize* a wrong behavior. This simply means that an action that is generally seen as *bad* becomes normal when allowed or repeatedly done by a group. Prime examples of this include bullying, drinking in excess, drugs, or trying cigarettes. Groups also impose penalties when a person doesn't conform to their decisions, by throwing them out of the group or turning a person into a social pariah.

How else does a group affect a person's thoughts, ideas, and emotions?

- Groups can magnify an idea or make an opinion more powerful. People feel confident when they join groups that validate their own opinions or thoughts. This is how labor unions, civic unions, or charities become so powerful and widespread. Think of it as little voices joining together to become a powerful one that can be heard all over by others.

- Leaders also have a huge impact on how a person thinks when that person forms a group. Leaders can steer groups in the direction they want to go or convince people to agree to certain ideas. There's no better example of this than politics.

The Problem of Face-ism

Face-ism is a problem that occurs often in society, although you may not realize it. It's basically when people make judgments towards a person based on their appearance but go beyond prejudice. This rests primarily on the face of a person—specifically the shape of the face. Face-ism states that simply based on the shape of a person's face, impressions are made about their personality. For example, studies show that features with a feminine appearance are often seen as extroverted. They're also seen as happier and more trustworthy. Does that mean that feminine features predict extroversion? No. It simply means when you see someone with very feminine features, you instantly label them an extrovert. But this doesn't have to be true and is just a predetermined way of thinking many are conditioned to believe.

I want you to distinguish between impressions on facial features and reading a person's body language. Impressions you make via facial features are stagnant or non-moving. Basically, this means that a person is not doing anything—their face is neutral. The impressions you get from their face are based purely on their blank features.

When reading faces and body language, however, we're looking at movement. People are reacting, doing, or thinking about something, and therefore causing their facial expressions and body to change in relation to what they're thinking or feeling. This movement is what we want to read here, not the blank expressions.

Physical Attractiveness

I hate to throw this out there, but beauty is a very strong motivator when it comes to reading body language, whether we like to believe it or not. And for negative or positive reasons. And I'm not just talking about people being generally attractive, pretty, or handsome. Even attractive features that you don't even notice at first can play a huge role in your ability to read their body language.

This includes features such as the shape of someone's face or their skin color, the clothes they're wearing, the perfume or aftershave they have on, or the style of their makeup. Don't think I'm just talking about people you find attractive that could take your breath away either.

Let's say you're talking to someone you've just met and you really like and you're just generally having a nice conversation with them. However, the wind blows and you catch the scent that they're wearing the same aftershave that your ex used to wear. You've got nothing against the person you're speaking with, but suddenly you're disconnected from the conversation because your mind is wandering. There's no way you're going to effectively read the conversation and listen properly because you're distracted.

It's only once you're able to bring your mind back to the present moment and focus that you'll be able to continue a grounded conversation. However, there's no doubt this attractiveness issue will occur when you're talking to someone you find attractive, such as when you're on a date.

As science shows, when you see someone you're attracted to, you get that rush of dopamine that makes you want to spend more time with someone, which can impair your logical decision-making ability. The same applies if you're talking to someone who finds you attractive.

Physical attractiveness can instill positive characteristics in a person that they haven't really lived up to. At the same time, being beautiful can also make it easier for an individual to distract you from their actual motives, depending on the nature of the person.

That all being said, being attracted to someone can make you read deeper into their superficial actions so that your interpretation would match your personal goals. For example, you might like someone and perceive a kind act as a flirtatious one when, in fact, they are acting perfectly normal in the given situation.

Your Mood Affects Your Reading Abilities

Another problem here is that your interpretation is affected by what you think or feel at that particular moment. If you're sad, then chances are you'll interpret the same thing in people. This is because you'll notice more cues and signs in other people who feel the same as you because your mind is on that level, both emotionally and physically. This is why when you surround yourself with infectiously happy people, you become happier yourself.

This isn't surprising since *reading people* effectively is basically you reacting to a situation, and reactions are hindered by overall mental and emotional health. This is why when reading people, it's important to try and maintain an unbiased view of things.

Now, this isn't always going to be possible. You may feel so sad, so hurt, so angry, or so excited and happy, that you just lose all thought and go into automatic. It happens to the best of us, and it's unavoidable. However, for the majority of the time, you want to enhance your focus, be present in the conversation, and be as mindful and as grounded as possible.

If you're forced to make a decision when you're feeling emotional, then ensure you're making a special effort to consider both sides of the story, take a good look at the different people involved, read them, and then make your decision. It's only smart to make readings when you're in a calm and collected frame of mind.

Like most of the strategies we're talking about throughout this book, this will come with practice. Sometimes you're going to get it right, and sometimes you won't, but the more you practice, the better at it you'll become.

The Advantages are Vivid

So, you're probably thinking, *with all these obstacles associated with reading body language, why should I even bother?*

Well, there are certainly obstacles to overcome and problems that you'll need to consider when reading someone's body language and improving your overall communication with them, the benefits are just as many—perhaps even more so.

Here are some of the benefits of being able to read a person's expression and body language:

You can connect better with people

This is the most important benefit listed here because this is really the result you want to get when reading this book.

To be able to look at a person and instantly find out what they feel or think can help you adjust your own response in order to help them, connect with them, love them, or progress with them. This is the sole point of communication. To connect effectively and genuinely

41

with other human beings without fear, anxiety, or stress.

One of our most basic human needs is to socialize and be social. To connect with others. To form deep and meaningful relationships with people. You've probably heard that being social is good for you, and it's true. Even science backs it up.

While the majority of studies on the benefits of social support have focused on the elderly (Steptoe, Dockray, & Wardle, 2009), having a robust social network is important both psychologically and physically at any age. For example, a study of incoming college freshmen revealed that social support was useful in lowering depression in both healthy and low self-esteem individuals (Cohen, Sherrod, & Clark, 1986). The authors of this study discovered that being a part of a social network helped people transitioning to university life feel less stressed.

As we get older, it's also crucial to stay socially active. Sirven and Debrand (2008) discovered that people who participated in social or communal activities were more likely to report good or very good health in a survey of Europeans over the age of 50. The study used data from the Survey of Health, Aging, and Retirement in Europe (SHARE), which comprised 22,000 families from 11 European nations (31,000 people).

On the flip side, while it's true that being able to be alone for short periods of time is healthy for an individual, being isolated for longer can be detrimental to your physical and mental health.

Also remember, you can feel lonely, even when you're physically surrounded by people. Happiness and satisfaction in life doesn't just rely on having people around you so you're not physically alone, but also on the quality of those relationships. This is why being connected with other people is so important!

Some of the dangers of being alone or feeling isolated include;

- Loss of memory or 'brain fog'. This is a symptom and danger that stems from the depression that can come from being isolated and alone. Some consequences of feeling this way include forgetting things, feeling confused, and making it hard to focus on anything.

- Headaches. Hand in hand with the consideration above, if you're feeling a lot of common headaches, then this could be a sign that you're feeling lonely. As we'll talk about in a second, this is because loneliness can lower your pain threshold since you're feeling depressed.

- Issues with digestion. Since loneliness and isolation is linked with stress, depression, and anxiety, it may come as no surprise that you'll experience digestive issues. When you feel panicking and your body enters flight or fight mode, you'll experience these symptoms tenfold.

- A weakened immune system. If you're feeling lonely, then the chances are you're feeling sick more often as well, and this is no coincidence. Studies show there's a very strong link between being isolated and alone and how often you feel ill. Loneliness has also been known to cause inflammation that damage and shut down your immune functions, thus making you more susceptible to illness.

- Tension in your muscles. Since loneliness causes physical stress on the body, you're much more likely to experience increased chronic pain or tension within your muscles which can be extremely painful, exhausting, and uncomfortable. Lower back pain is also very common.

- Reduced sex drive. Not a symptom you want to experience, and not just because you're on your own. When you're isolated for a long period of time, it lowers your sex drive, due to the depression-related side effects, which counter-productively pushes you further away from other people.

- Trouble sleeping. Sleep is affected by everything, especially when it comes to feeling isolated. You may find yourself having trouble falling asleep, oversleeping, feeling tired all day every day throughout the day, and not having enough energy at all. Again, these are all tied into feeling depressed which very commonly comes with feeling alone.

Tie all this together, and you see why it's so important to be proactive in forming deep and meaningful relationships with other people

As we've discussed, this is a skill that can be very useful in any social situation and will help you navigate through interactions with ease. Having an idea about what people think also lets you temper your conversation to make sure that no one is offended by what you said and cause you to communicate your own messages effectively.

In essence, you'll be able to get what you want in life!

You'll see improvement with your business or within your career

The workplace is packed with subtle, non-verbal manners of communication, and it can be very useful to know what's happening under the surface. Is the client interested in your presentation, or does he look completely distracted? You can take note of what pitches have a positive or negative reaction from your boss or client. With coworkers, having a good grasp on silent communication between people makes it easier to adjust to the demands of the office. At the very least, being able to read these subtle cues will tell you if you've made an impression in the office.

- *Help prevent conflict.* Another incredibly useful benefit of reading body language is conflict resolution. You can tell the silent signs of aggression before they actually occur, therefore allowing you to stop any negative action at just the right stage. This is useful in many situations from work, to parties, to disagreements with your partner. Knowing exactly when to defuse a situation before you reach that point of no return all starts with awareness.

- *Improve people's impression of you.* First impressions are always important, no matter what setting you're in. Knowing how to read body language doesn't just tell you how other people think, it also tells you how you're supposed to act in their presence. This means that you will be able to adjust people's impressions of you depending on a given situation. This is important if you want to create a strong presence in the office or if you want to keep things on the down-low during family gatherings. Knowing the time to spread out your arms or make yourself blend in with the background can definitely help in achieving the effects you want to have in a situation.

- *Become a better communicator.* Of course, if you're in the position to receive and interpret verbal and non-verbal communication, this puts you in the perfect place to respond to these same messages. Don't forget—communication is a two-way street, and in order to send a message in the right context, you have to be able to receive a message in the right context. Doing both correctly guarantees that the flow of information is stable, quick, and accurate.

As you can see, there are pros and cons to reading body language, but through awareness of this information, you can act accordingly. Bear in mind the weaknesses you may have when it comes to reading body language in your own life.

For me, during the peak of my social anxiety, I would find myself getting very emotional in situations. If someone at work made a passing comment, even with no harm meant, I would take it extremely personally. This almost always resulted in my being unable to read a situation properly because I was clouded by whatever emotions I was feeling.

Through research and experience, I learned that things didn't need to be this way, but I instead had control over how I could respond in any given situation. When I felt an emotion rise up, I could take a breather and choose to act accordingly rather than getting carried away with the emotions themselves. This is what it means to be an effective communicator. This applies to all points in both lists.

With this in mind, it's time to move to the next chapter where we're going to start learning some core strategies you can use in your day-to-day life when it comes to reading people of varying personalities and highlighting how to communicate with them more effectively.

Chapter 3: How to Identify and Communicate with Introverts

This chapter will delve deeper into personality types and how to make connections with people depending on their perceived personality types. I want to stress the use of the word *perceive* here because unless you've made them take a test to figure out their personality type, chances are you're going to be guessing what category they fall into. Again, the more experience you have in reading people, and the more familiar you are with these personality types, the more accurate you'll find yourself.

Practice makes perfect, people! This is why this chapter also helps you get to that point.

The best and most effective way to go about this is tackling the three issues in three ways. Again, we're going to try and make this as simple and as memorable as possible, despite there being a lot of information we could go into.

The three questions we're dealing with are;

1. How to identify someone's personality type, even when you've just met them
2. How do you communicate and connect with a specific personality type once you've identified it?

3. What is the typical motivation of this personality type?

Their motivation, I hear you ask?

Yes, after you're able to identify the sort of person somebody is, you then need to work on figuring out their motivation for the things they're saying, the actions they're doing, and what kind of aim they have with the interactions they're in. Now, don't take this as everyone has a secret motivation or aim that's making them act in a selfish manner. That just isn't true. What's your motivation when you hug someone when they're sad? Your motivation is to make them feel loved, happier, or more secure. There are always positive and negative motivations, but by identifying them within the people you're talking with, you're going to have a much better time reading them and their intentions.

Everyone has different motivations at different times in different situations. What's more, different personality types often have endgames or purposes when interacting with people. You will find that these different motivations can help you better figure out what they ultimately want in a given situation.

But we're going to be exploring all this over the following chapters. Instead, let's start with the basics of identifying someone with an introverted or extroverted personality type, and it's not what you think.

An introvert may not always be sitting in the corner of the room but may be in the center of action doing their best-extroverted act, vibing off the energy of others in the room. Remember how we spoke about how people will change their personality and won't be themselves because they're conforming to group pressures or are trying to hide who they actually are? We're exploring the techniques you can use to see through these masks and get to the truth.

But we won't stop there. After exploring introverted and extroverted types, we'll couple it with the Myers Briggs types in a little more detail, so when you're ready, let's jump in.

Signs of an Introvert

When it comes to identifying an introverted person, these are the signs you're going to want to keep an eye open for.

Zoning Out

In social situations, introverts are likely to zone out during conversations or in the middle of all the parties. They can easily become quiet during conversations as if they've mentally left the place. Don't worry, they'll come back sooner or later, often asking questions to help them catch up to the conversation.

A Finnish study back in 2016 found that extroverted people are far more likely to get a high from socializing in a similar way to introverted people, although their fatigue level hits around three hours after an introverted person does. In other words, introverted people get tired around people quicker and need some time to catch up!

They're the ones who leave early.

This doesn't happen just once but all the time during parties or social situations. This goes hand in hand with the study above. Introverted people are all about having their alone time to recharge!

Introverts are also the ones who tend to *disappear* during parties.

They're the ones who gravitate towards the quieter part of the house, often grouping up with other introverts and just talking quietly in a private space. Often, introverts stick close to the people they already know.

I remember going to house parties when I was a teenager and being an introverted type myself, I always seemed to find myself sitting outside on the patio or decking with a small group of people, rather than dancing and being loud with the large group of people in the main house. It's this kind of behavior that shows that someone is introverted.

But don't forget this doesn't just apply in an event setting, like a party. If someone is introverted at work, they will sit quietly on their own lunch, or tend to head off and do their own thing. Your partner may be introverted if they like to go off and spend time on their own.

Introverts seem to enjoy solitary activities more.

They're the ones who have an intense interest in books, the arts, or even the animals in the room. This kind of interest often allows them to be alone while still appearing as if they're enjoying themselves at the party.

There are many studies that back this up, perhaps the most popular being featured in a book titled 'The Secret Lives of Introverts' by Jenn Granneman. Throughout her book, she talks about how introverts require less social stimulation than extroverts and are more content with simple highs, like brief interactions and alone time activities, like reading and writing.

Again, this is because introverts are 'loners', or just don't like being around other people. Their brains are simply hardwired to get more dopamine from activities like this than an extroverted person will, who will get their dopamine hits from social interactions.

They can become quite irritable if socializing for long periods of time.

This is because introverts often need *downtime* after socializing for quite some time. Since introverts require time to recharge, it's like having an introverted or social hangover if they spend too long with other people.

They are happy when it comes to activities that let them be alone.

Hence, they can volunteer to serve the DJ, clean up the house, take food to someone, or even take photographs. This lets them stay clear from all the activities while still being part of the actual party.

Communicating with Introverts

When communicating with any person in this particular group, you want to remember that they're strong introverts. This means that their ability to maintain social communication is shorter—they often prefer their interactions to be quick and straight to the point.

Here are some of the things you have to remember when communicating with any of these types:

- Don't ramble, they hate that. If you want to communicate specific information, tell it to them straight.

- Do not use small talk if you want to get information from them. Ask about it straight out and you will get a straight answer from them.

- They may enjoy bantering, but if they're working on a particular project, it's important to stay away and just allow them to focus.

- Learn to listen because these types put a lot of stock into listening. Remember that their main goal is information so if someone is talking, they will make every effort to listen. Hence, they expect the same courtesy from others and hate it when people interrupt them in the middle of a sentence.

- Give them time to think about their answer before voicing it out loud.

- Greet them with a smile, but don't expect to stand there and exchange pleasantries. They're not really fond of that. Instead, greet them but give them their personal space. No hugs or any kind of air kisses unless you're very close or are a family member.

- Eye contact every now and then is okay simply to affirm connection. Don't overdo it, however. This can create a feeling of pressure.

- Do not rush them. Introverts like to enjoy their time working on a project. They're careful and particular about their goals and believe that distractions can lower the precision of their executions.

- When working with this type, it helps to always update them on what's going on. They want to find out at what stage you are in your job and not only when it's finished. This helps them assess the situation and adjust accordingly.

- Note that these types can go quickly from friendly to distant. They have a short social fuse which means that after some time socializing with others, they're going to need some alone time to recharge. True introverts, their social fuse tends to be shorter than most, unless they've managed to train themselves into it.

- During tense situations or when stressed, introverted types draw into themselves. They become quiet and stoic, unlike other types, which tend to burst out or let everyone know what they're feeling.

- Keep your greetings quiet and friendly. Try not to overload them with affection or be very public with your greetings. Make sure you're patient with the other person, giving them time to think and process the interaction.

  A Harvard study from back in 2012, conducted by Randy Buckner, found that the grey matter of the prefrontal cortex of an introvert is thicker and larger than that of an extrovert. This grey matter is linked with the decision-making processes. Since there's more matter, there are more processes happening, which could prove why they take longer to make decisions and process information.

- Don't rush things with them. Never interrupt; allow these types to fully say what they want to say before responding. Perhaps one of their biggest pet-peeves is being interrupted while in the middle of a sentence. Give nods every now and then to let them know you're following the conversation. This goes hand in hand with the information above!

- When push comes to shove, these personality types can become quite critical. That's okay, and not something you should take personally. Just relax and take on board what is being said from a neutral standpoint. Chances are they're just processing what is happening.

- Quality is more important than speed so be prepared to revise and rework your output several times before you'll get their approval. The same applies to conversations. Don't beat around the bush and carry on with small talk. Introverts like quality conversations, not quantity.

  This is backed by a study carried out by Inna Fishman in the Salk Institute for Biological Sciences in California. The study found that extroverted people are more sensitive to social stimuli than neutral stimuli, such as the weather or surrounding events. This means extroverts (surprise surprise) like socializing.

  On the other hand, introverts respond well to both social stimuli and neutral stimuli, basically stating that introverts don't need social interaction to feel good. The surrounding environment is just as stimulating, so make the conversations worth their while!

- Public recognition and compliments can be quite embarrassing and very uncomfortable for these types of people. While congratulations and celebrating accomplishments are good for anybody, keeping things small scale will deliver the best results.

As before, you're not expected to remember all this information, nor are you going to, but reading through some of the descriptions, you've probably thought to yourself *ah, that sounds like this person or that person,* so already you're starting to use the information.

With the communication strategies accompanying each section, try to tailor your communication accordingly.

Chapter 4: How to Identify and Communicate with Extroverts

Just like we did in the previous chapter, we're now going to take a look at the other end of the personality spectrum and dive into what makes an extrovert an extrovert.

Now, remember, you don't need to remember them all, but reading through these traits and descriptions are probably going to help you identify some of the people who are closest to you in your life and will equip you with the general knowledge you need to address and read other people.

Let's dive into the signs of an extrovert and highlight what you need to be on the lookout for.

Signs of an Extrovert

One thing I want you to remember is that extroversion is not a *bad* thing. There seems to be a current trend nowadays where introverts are viewed as the nice, sweet, unassuming people while extroverts are the gregarious ones who are flighty and talk too much. Note though that this isn't always the case. There is no *better* type and both introverts and extroverts have their own strengths and weaknesses.

Here are some of the typical distinguishing marks of an extrovert:

They have broad and numerous interests.

Extroverts are usually the types of people that encourage socializing and being with other people. Surfing, biking, and team games are some of the activities they usually enjoy.

They communicate best through conversations, rarely with writing.

In fact, they're very enthusiastic when talking, often adding punch to their argument through hand gestures. They're also comfortable showing affection in public. Hence, they're the types who will air kiss with friends, give people a slap on the back, and give shoulder hugs when they're happy.

They have no problem being the center of attention.

In fact, they can quickly lighten up when the attention is pulled towards them and such energy can make them feel more themselves, perpetuating them further. That doesn't mean that all extroverts are narcissistic. In fact, it's the opposite. If they're telling a story in a charismatic way to entertain others and become the center of attention naturally, they just have no problem with this, and probably won't even recognize it's happened, whereas an introvert would become very conscious of it.

They perform well in team settings.

They're happy with group work and can seamlessly blend with any group, regardless of the task. They are happy to communicate and lead and will be an integral part of any group or team effort.

They like going out on a routine basis.

They're the ones who may have a routine when it comes to nights out or drinks after dinner or work. Extroverts are likely to feel very disconnected and will suffer from loneliness symptoms far more regularly if their needs are frequently or consistently met.

They are comfortable expressing their thoughts and feelings out loud.

They will have no problem seeking out inspiration and advice from people they believe are capable of providing help.

How to Communicate with Extroverts

Since they're all extroverts, communicating with these personality types are more or less the same. Here are basic tips on how to forge connections with people in this category:

- Always smile and make eye contact when you greet them in the morning, or during whatever time you might see them. They're extroverts—they're happy to make that initial connection with you.

- Keep the energetic vibe up with gestures that are open and encompassing. Use your hands and arms, allowing for vibrant and obvious movements that encourage participation.

- Be responsive to questions asked and if you're the one asking the questions, keep them open-ended. Allow these personality types to expand on their answers or give them the chance to elaborate on the topic.

- They're the types who think out loud so let them rant out their thoughts before pitching in. This isn't them saying nothing out of thin air, it's actually their thought process.

- If you want to communicate information to them, then the best way to do that is to give personal examples or use stories. This will get their attention and make a better impact instead of just stating possibilities in a detached manner.

- Allow them to explore different options before arriving at a decision. Try not to pressure them into arriving at a conclusion, as this will only irritate them and lower the quality of their answer. Since they like to think out loud, allow them to rant it out before asking what their *final* thoughts on the matter would be. Do not assume the first thing they said is their answer because chances are they're just going through the instances in their head.

- If you want them to do something or are trying to convince them to be part of something, try pointing out something that you think would be fun or entertaining for them to do.

- There will be some debate and arguments when you're interacting with these personality types. Don't take it personally as this is their way of having fun.

- When trying to explain something to them, allow for more time when it comes to questions and conversations. Present the main points and let them ponder the information for as long as possible.

- Note that people with this kind of personality type tend to use humor during tense moments. This is their way of breaking the tense atmosphere.

  Take note that when angry or stressed, these personality types tend to become louder, more expressive, and heavily animated. It may seem completely out of context, but this is how they handle typical stressful situations.

- When greeting them, keep things friendly but allow them to talk. As you've probably gathered from the points above, extroverts like to talk, so give them the opportunity to do so. This includes not cutting them off or interrupting and allowing them to get to the end of their thoughts.

- Make direct eye contact when talking to them. Speak what you want to say quickly after thinking it through. Let them know what you want and why. They will appreciate this kind of discourse instead of running around the issue.

- Provide dopamine hits! Remember, extroverts can get mentally stimulated easily, so providing them with a challenge or activity can be a great way to excite them. Whether you're turning work into a game, asking a thoughtful question, or posing either a mental or physical challenge can be a great way to get them to engage.

One study by Michael X. Cohen concluded back in 2005 that extroverts receive far more dopamine far quicker than other people, usually instantly after a behavior has taken place (such as completing an action, getting a question right, and so on), or comes after a 7.5 second anticipation period.

An example of this in action would be saying something like, "I bet you can't print off your report in less than a minute." Then the intensity of the action takes place, and then not letting them know they won for about five seconds afterward the challenge is over is going to give them so much satisfaction. Psychology is weird, right?

- Positivity is everything! Extroverts who fall into this category love positivity because it gives them a wave to ride on. A simple 2010 study carried out at the Annual Convention of the American Psychological Association found that extroverts were far more mentally stimulated by pictures and images of people than introverts were, concluding that they place a far higher amount of importance on social connection.

  This then translates into the fact that if the said interaction that they were so excited about didn't go well, was awkward, or left a bitter taste in someone's mouth, this is going to crush the extrovert. Instead, keeping things positive is key!

- Be honest if you don't know the answer to a question. Tell them instead that you'll find out the answer as soon as possible.

- Don't be vague and interpret their words as is. If you already know exactly what they're telling you, then don't try to extrapolate on possible other meanings. If something is unclear, ask them outright. You should not be afraid about clarifying things with this type, as they prefer this to someone who just *guesses* on what needs to be done.

Okay, phew. That's a lot to handle.

I know that's a ton of information there, and don't worry, for the last time, you're not expected to remember it all, and nor do you need to. I include it because you can use this information as a reference to look back on if you ever want more information on someone specific in your life.

I would reread the actionable tips and see what jumps out at you and see which ways of communicating speak to you as an individual. For example, if you're communicating with an extrovert, but you're not the sort of person who feels comfortable talking about feelings or emotions, then you may want to get involved in activities instead as this will better form a connection.

It's important when steering the way you communicate with people that you're not actually becoming someone you're not. You don't need to pretend to be someone you're not nor just try to cater to being the person you think the other person wants you to be.

Effective communication is all about being true to yourself and who you are, but being able to read the other person and send your messages across to them in the way that will resonate best with them.

Think about certain people in your own life: your partner, your boss, your best friend, or your teenager and how these strategies can be applied in your own life and where improvements can be made.

For me, I struggled with my relationship with my boss. I didn't know how to present myself properly or get results. I had ideas, and I had all the drive to succeed on projects and with clients, but I could never seem to bring myself to take action.

Then, when I started learning about all these communications strategies, I concluded that my boss was an extroverted type, which meant he was decisive and confident and thrived on exploring new ideas and debating. For the first time in my life, I had read the personality of someone else.

I was then able to change up and have purpose in my conversational approaches. I would bring up new ideas and challenge his existing ones, finally coming to a quality conclusion that got results.

Over time, the respect from my boss grew because I was pushing all the right buttons, and eventually this way of thinking spread into plenty of other areas of my life. The results speak for themselves. Be your own proof.

But, alas, we must continue our journey. If you haven't already, I highly recommend doing a personality test yourself to see which one you are and how people can relate to you (www.16personalities.com) and trying to match people in your own life. Bookmark these chapters as well so you can come back any time!

Of course, the main point we're talking about is so you can communicate effectively with people in your life, so let's zero in on this in more detail as we dive deep into different communication types in this next chapter.

Chapter 5: Understanding and Identifying Communication Styles

I, and many people, define *communication style* as the way you exchange information with other people. There are basically four styles known today: passive, aggressive, passive-aggressive, and assertive. It's important to make a distinction between these four because the way information is communicated to you will affect how you respond to it and defines what the other person is trying to say.

This, of course, is a core strategy when it comes to reading other people and understanding their motivations.

The chances are you come across all four of these types of communication in everyone you meet, day in, day out, in one form or another, so becoming familiar with them is a powerful key that's going to unlock many doors when it comes to effective and meaningful communication. Don't forget that some people will use one style in one conversation, and change the next, so make sure you're fluid and not just labelling people and keeping them in a kind of identification box.

One thing you have to understand though is that you can't box people into single communication styles.

People also change the way they communicate based on the results they want to get and will change depending on their life situation and environment. In other words, someone who is usually quite passive can be aggressive if they're having a bad day. Basically, there are always going to be variables, which is why it's often best to classify the communication style as it comes.

Let's explore the different types of communication styles.

Passive

Passive communication is a form of communication where someone is speaking with a lack of assertiveness in what they're saying. In many cases, a passive person may even avoid saying what they think altogether or what they want because of the anxious thoughts telling them of the effect it may have.

I came across a good example of this the other day. I was sitting around a table in a diner with colleagues on our lunch break and the conversation moved onto politics. Of course, this can be a controversial subject to some, and while there were points for both Democratic and Republican views, I couldn't help but notice that a few people remained quiet. While they gave their points of view in little doses, they weren't strong points of view, and didn't really define what side of the fence they stood on. Instead, it was shaking or nodding their heads depending on what others said. They weren't sharing their own points of view.

There are plenty of reasons why they acted like this. They may hold a strong political opinion and be too afraid to share it out of fear of being judged or excluded from the group.

Another situation where this could be an example is when someone may love another person but is unwilling to share how they feel in case it's taken the wrong way. If conversations revolve around risk and reward, passive people are unable to take the risk, despite what the reward could be.

However, this method of communicating is in itself a style of communication, which means it can be read by you. The trick is to zero in on the person to figure out what hints they're giving away. Are you ready?

Here's where we start really diving into reading strategies.

When you're a passive communicator, you don't directly say something; you *hint* at it and just hope that the other person will get the hint. This can lead to all kinds of problems, such as miscommunication and situations that don't need to evolve.

Let's say you respond passively when you are on a date because you're shy and you don't want to scare the other person away. I've seen people do this countless times where they are usually a really outgoing, loud, and hyperactive person, but when they're meeting someone new they fancy or want to get on with, they tone themselves down so they don't give the impression they're really intense.

Remember, anyone can be a passive person at any time, and we all switch roles throughout our lifetime, depending on the situations we find ourselves in. Let's say you're this person, you're feeling passive and your date is asking where you want to go for dinner.

Usually, especially if you were with friends or family, you would say something like;

"Oh, I would kill for Chinese food right now. I'm so hungry!" But you're with your date, so you tone yourself down and become passive.

They suggest Thai food and you don't object, nor really say anything. You just agree and go along with it. You get to the Thai place, and, in reality, you hate Thai food and don't really eat much. Because of this, your body language gives off all the unconscious messages that you're not having a good time and not enjoying yourself, thus the date goes badly, and you never see each other again. Ouch.

That doesn't mean that there's not a time and place for being passive. Sometimes if someone is mad and acting mindlessly, you'll want to be passive because you need to wait for them to calm down so you can actually have a grounded conversation.

People can be passive for all kinds of reasons. They might be having a bad day, they may feel intimidated or scared of someone in the surrounding area (think a child unable to speak their mind because they're scared of what their parents might think), or just don't have a strong opinion and feel it's worthless to say anything.

The point is, how can you still read someone and what they're trying to say?

How do you know when someone is trying to tell you something different from what they're actually saying? Fortunately, there are signs you can think about. Passive communication usually has the following body language tells:

- Lack of eye contact or in some cases, extreme, excessive eye contact

- Dropped shoulders and hunched back

- Keeping their head down

- A low or quiet voice

- Emphasizing certain words

- May repeat basic sentences in an effort to communicate what they're trying to say

- May say phrases like: "It really doesn't matter" or "As long as everyone is happy"

- They tend to go with the flow

How to Communicate with Passive Communicators

The main problem you'll face when communicating with passive people is the fact that they don't want to come out of their shells. They either lack confidence or don't have the degree of self-worth where they end up believing that their opinions, thoughts, and perspectives aren't valid, and nobody wants to hear them.

As an effective communicator yourself, the trick here is to boost the self-worth of a passive individual and help to coax them into opening up. The simplest way to do this is simply to ask them what their thoughts are on a subject.

You could say something like "Hey, what do you think?"

If someone has a hard stuck habit of being passive, they may respond with something like, "Oh. Me? Nothing." This is where you'll respond with something like "Come on, you can tell me. I'm genuinely interested in what you have to say."

To make this easier, here's a step-by-step guide you can follow when talking to someone who's passive.

Step 1: When communicating, ask a passive individual how they feel or what they are thinking.

Because they may not be able to express themselves honestly, it's critical to pull them out of this mindset by affirming what they say in order to develop a trusting and mutually respectful environment.

Even if you disagree with what they're saying, it's not about being right or wrong, or putting someone down for their beliefs. Proper communication is about understanding and connecting with the other person, regardless of the actual content of what they're saying.

Once connected, then you can really start to grow and

nurture an actionable relationship. This means you need to acknowledge the parts of what they are saying that are important and always express your gratitude for hearing those thoughts.

You may say something along the lines of: "What you're saying intrigues me much. I'd like to learn more about it."

Make sure you repeat the key points of what's being said, because this shows you've listened to what they said and you're taking onboard their points of view. The more listened to you can make someone feel, the better you'll connect.

Step 2: When interacting with a passive person, pay attention.

Interrupting or belittling the person you're talking with is a bad idea since it discourages free dialogue. After all, if someone kept doing that to you, then you would feel put down and disrespected and as though your points are worth listening to. This will be counterproductive when trying to get someone to connect with you.

A way around this and to prove you're listening and paying attention is, in a few words, summaries what they are saying.

"If I understand you correctly, you are saying that...," you can say, and then repeat what they said in your own words. Paraphrasing will show the passive person that you care about what he has to say.

Step 3: Be conscious of your nonverbal signals and body language.

Make sure you're aware of what your body language is saying. This is a point that applies when communicating and reading someone speaking in any communication style, but specifically with passive people because closed-off gestures and body language is only going to make them feel even more shut out.

Closed gestures include crossing your arms, frowning, and looking away from the individual since these are all primal defense measures used by a person before an assault.

Closed gestures provide a nonverbal indication to a person that you've shut down and aren't listening to what he's saying.

Instead, make open nonverbal gestures like smiling, relaxing your posture, and keeping your arms at your side.

Open gestures do not communicate to the other person that you are defending yourself against an impending attack; rather, they communicate to the passive person that you are comfortable and willing to listen to what he has to say.

Step 4: Acknowledge any effort made by the passive individual to convey feelings.

In the long term, both of you will be happier if there is open communication with both of you expressing your wants.

Praise has a favorable influence on persons with low self-esteem and will assist the passive person link nice feelings with her experience with you. Even saying something like, "Thank you for sharing," can be enough acknowledgement to validate how someone feels and to help encourage them to come out of their shell a little more.

Step 5: Use assertive behavior by resolving disputes quickly and directly.

Conflict often goes unresolved because a passive individual prefers to avoid confrontation, and therefore just stays quiet. If you're in this situation, then it's important to address any difficulties directly but by making sure you do so in a courteous manner. This includes making an effort to applaud any cooperative efforts they have made.

You may say something like, "I don't want to fight or argue. I really want us to work together to find a solution to this problem that benefits everyone."

Summary of Passive Communication

It takes time and energy to get someone to open up, but it's not impossible. They may be scared of being judged (think about a child afraid of sharing their opinion because they feel their parents may judge them negatively for it), or even intimidated by other people in the interaction. Even in situations like this, boosting someone's confidence by acknowledging them and then validating what they're saying is the best way to help them to open up and communicate. It's all about the balance of respect, compassion, and empathy.

On that note, it's important to remember not to try to force someone to open up if they really don't want to, thus becoming an aggressive communicator yourself. This isn't going to benefit anyone and is only going to push the person into becoming more passive. If someone doesn't want to open up, accept this and move on. You can always try again another time. The more consistent you are, the more likely they'll be to increase their confidence in themselves and you thus open up, eventually.

This means when you're talking to a passive person, you need to validate what they're saying, make them feel heard, repeat keywords back to them to prove it, and acknowledge them and what they're saying.

Body language, such as keeping eye contact and nodding for them to continue what they're saying, is key in situations like this.

Aggressive

Aggressive communication isn't something you can just ignore, usually because you're being forced to hear what they have to say. If someone communicates information in an aggressive manner, you will be able to tell.

Aggressive communication is usually the result of an emotional person and doesn't have to mean a violent or tempered interaction (although it certainly does include this), it can also revolve around someone who is stubborn, unwilling to change their opinion, or is forceful with their perspective.

Additionally, aggressive communication usually comes with a lack of compassion and empathy because the person is more focused on trying to force their point of view, rather than respecting and listening to others. It can be hard to deal with someone who's aggressively communicating, and relationships commonly tend to suffer because of it.

This style has the following signs:

- A loud and demanding voice
- There are threats, criticisms, blaming, intimidation, or any other tactic to compel you into doing what they want
- Aggressive posture and forceful body language
- Intense eye contact

Aggressive communication isn't so much about conveying information but rather, telling a person what they should do with little regard for what anyone else has to say or think. It can also signal a lack of patience or show signs of stress. Remember, someone could be acting aggressive because they are being defensive, and they're trying to protect themselves from a perceived threat.

However, aggressive communication isn't always a

negative thing as aggression can be interpreted as a great sign of leadership if used in a productive way that helps the objectives get reached in the best possible way. It can extend to confrontations or telling people exactly what they think without regard to circumstances, reactions, or feelings.

How to Communicate with Aggressive Communicators

It's very difficult dealing with aggressive communicators because when someone is acting this way, they are only thinking of themselves and their own points of view. Rarely are they thinking about you, your perspective, or how they feel. It's all about gaining power and control of the situation, whatever the cost.

Now, remember, there are many reasons why someone would be aggressive. If you're unlucky, this is just the nature of the person, perhaps from previous trauma in life, but whether someone is suffering or just having a bad day and taking it out on everyone else, the main reason someone will be aggressive is that they're being defensive.

Dealing with aggression like this is hard work, and you only have a few options. The first and perhaps most important thing to remember is that you can leave the situation.

Let's say you're arguing with your partner about something trivial and things get heated. It happens. Emotions are heightened and stressful feelings cloud judgments. Your partner is aggressively communicating because they don't feel heard or acknowledged. Usually, the best way to deal with this is to give the conversation room to breathe.

Whether you're going to physically leave the room to allow everyone to calm down, go for a walk, or even go to bed and sleep on the situation, allowing time for a bit of space can do wonders for allowing the dust to settle. When you come back to the conversation, everyone can be refreshed in a more balanced state of mind.

However, sometimes you'll need to remain in the conversation with an aggressive person, so here's some tips on how to deal with them, and remember, fighting fire with fire will simply exacerbate the situation and encourage the other person to become more aggressive.

Step One: Maintain your composure.

Take a deep breath in and out. Get out of your chair to get a glass of water or to check your phone. Whatever it is you do, doing something different relieves the strain that has been building up throughout the conversation.

If you match the person's aggression, get defensive, take it personally, or get aggressive and rage-filled in your own way, consider how much you'll regret the things you say. Always aim to stay as calm as possible and maintain your composure. Doing anything else will only make the situation worse.

Step Two: Call attention and focus on them.

Be direct and to the point with aggressive people. If you

beat around the bush, you're not going to get anywhere. You need to call it as you see it in an honest and truthful way.

Don't act as if nothing is upsetting you during the talk. However, rather than aggravating the other person even more, you should point out that they are being aggressive with a sympathetic statement.

Instead of using the words 'you' or 'your,' try something like this:

- 'Don't worry, we'll figure it out.'
- 'Could you kindly lower your voice.'
- 'I'm sorry, can I say something important/helpful?'
- 'I understand this can be stressful/upsetting.'

Remember, aggressive doesn't necessarily mean angry. If someone is incredibly upset or hurt, this could be defined as aggressive communication because they're locked into their own way of thinking.

If you do this early on, it will help them break free from their state of unawareness and become more mindful of their actions. As a result, the person may be more receptive to whatever you have to say.

Step Three: Empathize and Be Compassionate

Put yourself in the shoes of the other person and attempt to comprehend why he or she is acting aggressively. Aggression is a natural reaction to protect or claim something, however, it can still be difficult to actually empathize with someone who's acting this way.

Consider the following topics to help with this part of the process:

- What is there for the other person to lose? (Time, money, friends and family, status, and reputation, among other things)

- What would you think if you found yourself in such a situation?

- Is there something else going on in the person's life that causes him or her to be irritable and irritable all of the time?

Step Four: Be Assertive Yourself

It may seem counterintuitive to be both sympathetic and assertive, yet the two are not mutually exclusive. That doesn't mean you're laying down the law and making the other person shut up or remain quiet, but you're staying true to yourself. The worst thing you can do is become passive.

Understanding the other person's point of view does not imply that you will tolerate their harsh behavior.

Step Five: Maintain a quiet and steady tone of voice.

This will demonstrate confidence and will not encourage the other person to speak louder than you.

Keep your cool and don't let the person dominate the conversation. Don't be afraid to express yourself. Maintain a respectful demeanor and expect the same in return.

If the level of violence rises, respond with greater force and assertiveness to demonstrate that your tolerance is dwindling.

Remain cool, calm, collected, and in control, and this is how you'll be able to successfully deal with an aggressive person.

Passive-Aggressive

The passive-aggressive manner of communication is perhaps the most frustrating for both the sender and the receiver. It's a subtle combination of the two previous communication styles, allowing a person to appear passive on the surface but with a hint of aggressiveness under the layer of passivity.

We all know someone at some point in our lives who has been passive-aggressive, perhaps coming across as being sarcastic with what they're saying. Recently in my own life, I saw a coworker who was passive aggressive towards another coworker who won a contract that they wanted to have.

The jealous coworker was saying things like "Yes, oh my god, the project was amazing, and they did such a wonderful job." On paper, this looks like a nice thing to say. But, couple their actual tone of voice while saying it, with what they said, and it was clearly aggressive while trying to keep a straight face.

What are the typical signs of this communication style? Watch out for these:

- Muttering under their breath instead of confronting a person
- Verbally agreeing but doing something else entirely
- Denying the existence of a problem despite body language showing opposition or reluctance
- Silent treatment or sarcasm
- Spreading rumors or talking behind someone's back
- Saying things like, "I'm okay with it, but someone else may not like it."

The problem is that passive-aggressive people are on the defense. These are people who often feel powerless and stuck in their situation. In the case of my coworker, she really didn't like that she didn't get the project, but there was nothing she could do about it. Thus, she resorts to passive-aggressive attitudes because she feels like she has no other option. Like aggressive communication styles, she's clouded by her emotions. Don't worry, I'm sure we've all been like this at some point, and perhaps will again. It's all about looking out for the signs and moving forward productively.

How to Communicate with Passive-Aggressive Communicators

Just like the other negative communication styles, passive-aggressive communication can be hard to deal with, mainly because the person is defensive and mourning a lack of control in a given situation. The best thing you can do here is to remain assertive (see below).

This means you need to stick to being you. You voice your opinion and thoughts, and you remain respectful of the other people within the interaction. This means you remain honest and open and recognize the fact that fighting fire with fire is only going to spread the blaze further. Use these interactions as an opportunity to practice your patience and empathy.

The most important thing to remember, similar to how you deal with all these communication styles, is to remain calm, not to let their words get under your skin, and to not take things personally. As soon as you bite and allow emotion to take you over, it's game over and the situation is only going to get worse.

Of course, if someone is passive aggressive on a regular basis, then there comes a time where you'll need to set boundaries that limit the amount of time you're spending around this person, just to preserve your sanity!

Assertive

Of all the communication styles, this is perhaps the best one as well as being the most effective. Assertiveness is a manner of communicating what you want to say without hurting anyone's feelings. You get to say what you want to say, sharing your views and opinions, but you also have the respect and empathy to listen to others and take on board what they're saying. It's all about being yourself, yet not forcing yourself down someone's throat, but rather taking onboard other people's point of views and being the best version of yourself in all fields.

Now, if you're surrounded by friends and family who all share similar opinions and perspectives, it's not hard to be assertive because you're all already on the same page.

However, you're not always going to be around other people who are on the same page as you, and you're frequently going to come across people who think differently. This is obviously the case with reality, and it's needed because if we all thought the same, life would be boring and uncreative. However, to communicate with other people, you need to practice being assertive.

Being assertive means having open and productive communication with another person, allowing both of you to express your thoughts, ideas, feelings, desires, and needs—without causing unnecessary friction. The goal is to create a balance so that all parties come out of the conversation content.

How do you do this? An assertive communicator has the following characteristics:

The primary way to be more assertive in conversations is actually fairly easy. You simply need to use 'I' more in what you say. Contrary to what you may think, this does not translate as selfishness but simply validates what you feel without putting blame on other people. Words like "I feel frustrated" or "I feel helpless" are used (rather than a phrase like it's helpless) which allows other people into your thoughts, giving them room to adjust and empathize with your situation. It allows you to claim ownership over what you feel and the behaviors that go along with that feeling, as well as opening the door for someone else to share how they feel.

Some of the key signs to look out, or ways to become more assertive yourself, include;

- Maintain connective contact. Contact can be in the form of eye contact or if you're comfortable with it, physical contact. The confidence you have with the other person helps you to carry what you're saying.

- Smile and assume a positive posture. Listen to what people have to say but make sure that you get your own time to speak. It's all about having a balance between listening and speaking, and not just acting as though you're listening, but actually hearing what the other person has to say and making an effort to understand them and to make them feel heard.

- Make sure to address any objections on a point-by-point basis. Repeat what they said and address each one individually until you've tackled all the issues raised. You can then present your own points of view, provide the benefits for them, and bring forth a call to action to encourage people to join in. If you're unsure of what someone said, then ask them questions. This is another great way of showing them you're listening.

- Keep your tone calm and low without any hint of smugness or superiority. In many cases, people resist new ideas simply because of the speaker or the way the new idea is introduced in a conversation. You want to make it as gentle and as friendly as possible to help people be more welcoming to the idea.

Now, with that list completed, we come to the end of this chapter. Hopefully, you're feeling very familiar with the communication styles that are out there and you know what to look for, how to identify the communication style of others, and how to choose what kind of communicator you want to be yourself.

It's time to move onto one of the areas of communication I find most interesting, and that's figuring out whether the messages that people are giving you are honest or not. In other words, we're going to explore how to tell when people are lying.

Chapter 6: Reading Lies in People

One of the most valuable skills when reading people is being able to tell when they're lying. Admit it—you've always wanted to know when someone is lying to you, and what a skill it would be. The number of opportunities it would open for you to know the truth.

I worked in sales for many years, and we would frequently be up against other companies trying to score contracts and negotiate deals. While I must stress it's not as glamorous as it sounds, it was a fantastic opportunity to improve myself while adapting my people skills, like communication.

In the case of honesty, there were frequent situations where I would be talking to clients or competitors about contracts, and it would be evident that they were lying. *No, we're sticking with your company. We're not looking anywhere else. Yes, we can get the work done by such-and-such date. No, this is all the budget we can afford for this project.* The list is literally endless.

But surely people don't lie that often? Sure, people will tell white lies every now and then, and everyone will tell a big lie for seemingly no reason at least once in their life, but surely this can't be a skill you'll want to invoke very often? Why bother learning it if not?

Well, it turns out that studies and questionnaires found

that around 40% of people admit to lying at least twice per day. As it turns out, around 90% of children will have learned how to lie by the age of four and 90% of people will lie on their dating profiles whether through straight up dishonesty or exaggeration.

Studies show that 80% of women will tell 'half-truths' frequently, 13% of patients lie to their doctors, 30% of people lie about their diet and exercise schedules, and 70% of people who lie would tell the same lie again if given the chance.

The statistics go on like this, but to round it all up, the average American will lie around 11 times per week, so just under twice per day. This means you're probably being told far more lies than you first thought, which is why having the skills to read them and spot them out can benefit you so greatly in your day-to-day life.

While the trick to telling if someone is lying may seem like a superpower, there's no mind-reading or special abilities involved. In fact, the method for detecting falsehoods is really quite simple. There are several ways you can go about it, but there is one that relies solely on your ability to read body language.

And as we've discussed already, reading body language is a skill that can be improved over time and is something you can get better and better at, so this method fits into this practice perfectly.

You've probably heard this before, but studies have proven countless times that when someone is lying, people have specific *tells*. This could include movements such as scratching their nose or brushing their hair with their fingers.

People who play poker often use these *tells* to see if they should match the other person's bet and take a risk on their hand. If you head over to YouTube and search "example of poker tells", there are several videos that show you things to look out for that are specific to the game. For example, someone raising the stakes may instantly start playing with their chips, their mind trying to occupy itself naturally while attempting to convince someone of their lie. The mind works in a strange way. It tries to distract itself from thinking about the fact that it's telling a lie in case it creates a tell, but in doing so, creates a tell.

This psychological *tell* can be found everywhere in nearly everyone in all aspects of life, and it's understanding and being able to identify these tells that we're going to be exploring throughout this chapter.

One thing I want to remind you of is that reading lies in a person is not an exact science. People's actions when lying can vary, which is why familiarity with the person is important. The longer you know a person, the more accurate your prediction will be about the truthfulness of what they're saying.

So, that being the case, here are the typical signs of lying according to experts.

Understanding a Baseline

One thing I want you to remember is that when reading body language, there's usually a *baseline* that allows you to start somewhere. A baseline is simply the *normal* way in which an individual acts when around other people. Simply put, if a person is being truthful and confident in their usual surroundings, how exactly do they act? What are their behaviors? What does their body language look like? Of course, there are both some general things to look out for that you can see in anyone, and characteristics that suit people individually, so it pays to know what to look out for.

Knowing a person's baseline lets you know when they're acting out of character. Sure, you can walk into a room full of strangers and do a casual *read* of the room, but reading people close to you is often easier as you've known them for a longer period of time. You have a point of reference, to put it simply.

Some people just love to talk with their hands to exaggerate what they're saying, while other people just love to fidget with their hair, even on normal days when they're just being honest. Just because someone is playing with their hair, that doesn't mean it's a tell if it's something they do regularly anyway. Hence, seeing them do this doesn't automatically mean they are lying, it might simply be a part of their personality. However, when someone who doesn't play with their hair a lot does this, this could be a telltale sale.

So, as you spend time with people in your life, be it friends, family, or coworkers, start to observe how they act normally and how they carry themselves. When they do someone out of the ordinary, you'll know something is up.

But how do you actually baseline someone? Based on the tips lined out by experts in the lie spotting project and studies run by some of the best psychological experts in the field, including ex and former CIA and FBI agents, here are some tips to follow.

Start Baselining from Day One

From the moment you meet someone for the first time, you'll need to start baselining someone, but don't worry, this is easier said than done. Our brains baseline people automatically all the time. Even if you see someone infrequently, say the girl on the front desk at the gym, you've been baselining her from the moment you met, and while you may only see each other for five minutes, the chances are you'll be able to tell when she's having a good or bad day, just from her behaviors and the way she speaks.

The trick is now to start baselining them mindfully from day one. This means monitoring their first impression, even from the moment they are walking up to you. Say you're walking into a meeting. Baseline everyone in the room and see how you feel. Trust your gut instinct because it will tell you who to look out for and who is doing what.

Ask yourself some of these questions:

- Does the person look alert and formal or casual?
- What emotions do their facial expressions say they're feeling?

- How stressed does the other person look?

- Do they look comfortable in the environment and who they're with?

- Do they look busy?

- What clothes are they wearing?

- Do they look engaged or distracted?

- Do they look tired?

- Do they look athletic?

You can ask yourself any questions to start building up a picture with what someone is like. Remember, this isn't invasive to monitor the people you're interacting with. Why wouldn't you? If you saw a guy shouting to himself in the street, you'd probably want to avoid this person because they're clearly exhibiting unstable behavior. You're reading this person and making conscious decisions.

As before, the brain does all of this unconsciously anyway. This process is just about bringing a bit of mindfulness to it and then using this information to your benefit.

Start Asking Questions

If you're unsure about anything, or if you're looking to dive in deeper into what something is thinking, feeling, or doing, but make sure you're doing this in a way that actually creates results. For example, if you're meeting someone at a funeral for the first time, you're not going to try and baseline them by telling jokes.

What you can do is do things like share a surprise compliment, say something a little out there, or gently challenge what someone is saying. This will create a response that you can use to baseline them. This can feel like you're generalizing, but it works because people really don't change that much.

For example, if someone is talking about a current news affair and you politely challenge their opinion, do they look interesting and ready to debate in a meaningful conversation, or do they suddenly withdraw? Do they get defensive or even aggressive? It's these little behavioral indicators that you want to look out for.

Other things to look out for include;

- Vocal tone of voice and speaking speed
- Standing and sitting postures
- Laughing style
- Any nervous tics
- Hand gestures
- Eye contact

Remembering the Details

After all this, the most important thing to remember is that you need to remember these baselining details. After all, what's the point? Sure, this may not be necessary if you're meeting with someone for the first time and you're never seeing them again, but we are talking about spotting liars in your life, so the chances are these are people you're going to see more than once.

While it may seem excessive to write down the behaviors you've observed after a conversation with someone, the act of doing this can massively help you process what you're picking up, especially when you're just starting out on this journey of reading people.

Personally, I got into the habit of writing down notes on my phone of body language signs and behaviors I noticed in people I spoke to, like my partner, my boss, and friends. These were only little bullet pointed, one-word observations, and I deleted the note a few minutes after writing them down, but this act of mindfully writing everything down helped me remember the signs indefinitely.

If you can keep repeating this process of most people in your life, it will start to be someone you do without thinking, and something you'll be more and more accurate at doing. However, this isn't everything. This is just one strategy you'll want to tie in with the others when it comes to reading people, and in this case, figuring out when someone is lying to you.

For the rest of this chapter, let's take a look at some of the other body language signs and tells you need to look out for when communicating with anyone.

Observe Hand Movements

People who are lying tend to use gestures, but they do it after speaking. Typically, you'd find people gesturing while talking because this is a natural part of the process. Their body is working with the mind in telling a story or conveying a message.

In contrast, a person lying is focusing too much on making up the story that the body fails to catch up. Hence, they make up the lie first and then perform the gestures to emphasize their point. Also, take note that gestures of people who are lying often involve both hands as opposed to truthful people who only use one hand.

Back in 2015, the University of Michigan broke down 120 video clips of important court cases to see how people behaved when they were lying versus when they were telling the truth. The study concluded that people use both hands to exaggerate their truth in 40% of cases, whereas only 25% of people use both hands while telling the truth.

This is a sign that excessive hand gestures while speaking is a sign of dishonesty.

Another unconscious body language done by dishonest people is keeping their palms away from you. This is a subliminal way of holding information away from other people that most people will do unconsciously during conversations, so keep an eye open for it. Hence, they may put their hands in their pocket or keep them close to their body, as if they're trying to keep something a secret inside their palms. So basically, people who lie can go two ways with their hands: they can either use them too much or not at all. Look for the extremes.

Itching and Fidgeting

There's a popular belief that when a person lies, they tend to scratch their nose. It's only one of the most stereotypical poker tells out there. Of course, this isn't true 100% of the time for every single person since everyone is different—but it does bear noting in many cases, this could be a surefire tell.

The fact is that it's fairly normal for people to have an itching sensation or fidget in their seat when they're uncomfortable; the body naturally looks for a way to distract itself while trying to avoid getting caught. Research carried out by UCLA by Dr. Lillian Glass and professor R. Edward Geiselman has concluded similar results in this field of research. Also note that when lying, people are often nervous about what they're saying, which causes the autonomic nervous system to fluctuate thus creating that tingling sensation all over the body. It's a lot like the nerves you get when you sit close to someone you like during those younger days.

However, nose scratching isn't the only itching movement associated with lying. When people lie, they play with their hair, play with their fingers, scribble on a notebook, or perhaps the most go-to technique nowadays—they play with their phones. Whatever the tell, when someone is talking to you and they start acting restless, this could be a sign that they're not telling the truth. You see it all the time in children who are lying to their parents about not taking chocolate biscuits when they shouldn't have and other such events. They twiddle their fingers in their palms and can't make eye contact. These behaviors continue throughout our lifetime.

Facial Expressions

Of course, let us not forget how the face itself can signify when someone is lying.

The eyes in particular can tell you so much depending on when a person chooses to look at you and when they choose to look away. Looking too much or not looking at all can be indicative of lying. Some people prefer to meet your gaze when lying because they *think* this will impress upon you their sincerity. They do say the eyes are the windows to the soul.

Commonly, non-experienced liars tend to look away when uttering a lie. They feel as though they can't bear to look at you in case of getting caught and something will give them away, when in fact this refusal to act normal says it all. But the same does work in the reverse, aka, staring.

The same 2015 Geiselman UCLA study I mentioned above researched this as well. In the court clips, over 70% of people who were lying would stare at the people they were lying to. Again, when trying to read someone, you're looking for the extremes. Too much staring or a complete lack of eye contact will be a dead giveaway. However, it's granted that this can be a little confusing when judging people simply through their eyes. This is why it's important to have a baseline when it comes to people, as we spoke about already.

One thing I want you to remember, though, is that a 2012 study published by *PLOS One* has already debunked the popular myth about where a person looks when lying. The myth goes that when a person is fabricating something they look left and when they're recalling something, they're looking right. This is not true as the direction people look is largely based on their mannerisms. That being the case, try not to focus too much on the direction but instead simply on the overall mannerisms of the individual you're communicating with.

Change in Complexion

This one's pretty obvious, and you've probably heard of it before or have seen it for yourself. Look for skin color and complexion changes. People blush, people become red or become pale depending on the circumstances. People tend to become pale when they're nervous or afraid of something. When the skin turns a shade of red, however, that can also be indicative of anger or perhaps even excitement, like when a teenager typically blushes when sitting beside their crush. Basically, if you read a change in skin color, you know something's up, so use this as a sign to look deeper into what the other person is thinking.

Sweat in the T Zone

This is something you definitely have to watch out for when wondering if a person is lying to you or not. The T

Zone is an area of the face that spans up across the forehead, down the nose, and onwards towards the mouth. Sweating is fairly common in this area if a person is lying, especially if they're nervous about it.

Tone of Voice

While we're focusing a lot on non-verbal communication here, the tone of voice is still a strong indicator of whether someone is telling the truth or not, absent from the words themselves. High-pitched voices tend to come out of nervous people as the vocal cords tighten, making it hard to push out the particular words. There can also be a croak, a stutter, or some broken words coming out of a nervous individual. Some people clear their throats to help improve their speech, which is also indicative of nervousness. In contrast, a loud and booming voice can be a sign of confidence or anger, depending on the situation. A sudden change in the volume can also indicate defensiveness in people, especially when confronted with possible mistakes.

The Mouth

Playing with the lips, such as rolling them back until they almost disappear, is another good indicator, as well as biting a lip. It's typically a sign of lying by omission as people physically try to hold back a word or a thought by pulling in their lips. If it goes the other way, however, it can be a sign of resistance or when a person doesn't want to talk about something.

The Words Themselves

Again, we're trying to focus on the non-verbal way of communicating, but I still want to cover all bases. After all, experienced liars can easily control their body language to match the situation. Hence, you still have to listen to the words themselves as they can indicate when a person is trying too hard to convince you of their truthfulness. Some common phrases used by liars include:

- "Honestly..."
- "Let me tell you the truth..."
- "Uh..."
- "Like..."
- "Um..."

Understanding How a Lie Works

One of the most interesting facts I ever read was that people who are lying spend way more energy on presenting themselves in a truthful way and trying to hide their tells that they spend energy on the actual story itself. Telling lies in such a way is incredibly taxing on a person's cognitive system because they're creating a story out of nothing, even if the story or lie is a simple one by nature.

One way to overcome this is simply to ask the person you think is lying to you to tell you the same story but in reverse chronological order. Since the person has spent so much energy trying to get away with the lie, the chances are they've skipped over the details and won't be able to remember them properly.

This technique is backed by a scientific study conducted back in 2008 aptly named *Increasing cognitive load to facilitate lie detection: The benefit of recalling an event in reverse order*. Within the study, a false, staged situation was created in which 80 people either told the truth or told lies. Some people were told to retell the events in chronological order, and others in reverse. The liars telling the story in reverse found it much more difficult and were easier to spot than any other group.

Your Gut Instinct Knows All

This final consideration is perhaps the most important. You ever just get that gut feeling that something isn't right, and the person you're speaking with is lying to you? Yeah, we all get that feeling from time to time. It's like standing at the end of a dark alley on your way home alone late at night and you get that strong feeling that, no, you're not going down there tonight. You're going to take the well-lit street down the road. This is your natural human instinct in full effect.

It's important to remember that your human instinct is incredibly powerful when it comes to things like this because it knows every human interaction you've ever had and will be able to pick up on tells and signs of dishonesty, even if you can't consciously place your finger on what is wrong.

A 2014 study in unconscious lie detection published in Psychological Science set up a situation where 72 people watched videos of fake crime suspects who were accused of taking a $100 bill off a bookshelf. Some people had taken it, whereas others had not. All the suspects had been told to state that they had not taken the money.

While the method proved to be inconsistent, with liars being identified 43% of the time, and truth-tellers identified 48% of the time, this was when people were given a time frame to think and observe the footage. In the time-restricted trials, where participants had to give quick-reaction answers based on what they saw, the participants would unconsciously use words like *dishonest* more frequently when the person was actually lying, and words like *honest* when people were telling the truth.

In other words, there's a very high chance your initial gut reaction going into a social interaction is right, so bear it in mind and be mindful of how you feel when identifying a liar.

Chapter Summary

Phew. That's a lot of information.

I remember when I first learned some of these tactics after completing a body language and charisma course during my early twenties, and I was astounded with how well they worked. Like I said before, the more you know someone, the more of a baseline you have of them, the easier they'll be to read because you'll be able to spot the clear differences in their characters.

However, with this knowledge in your mind, and with some experience, you can even spot these signs in strangers you've only just met. While humans are so different, we are all similar in so many ways, especially when it comes to basic psychology and how our brains work; aka tells and reacting in certain ways when certain things happen.

Keep an eye out for these signs in people you interact with, or perhaps even try lying to your friends (let them know this is the plan, you don't want to fall out with anyone.) One of my favorite games to play while walking in the city with my family is saying three statements, two are true and one is false, and everyone else has to guess which is false. It's a great way to practice and a lot of fun.

Of course, you can't just rely on one sign. Usually a person will showcase two or three. This is essential because if you're spotting more than one, then this is more likely to confirm that they're being dishonest.

Now we're going to dive into something new, another of my favorite topics, which is understanding the motivations and drive behind people when they are communicating. What do they want and why are they saying what they are saying? Are there hidden,

underlying messages something we should be aware of?
Let's find out.

Chapter 7: Understanding People's Motivations

In the previous chapter, we talked about lying and how to tell when someone is lying to you. If you ever watched one of my favorite television series, *House*, you may remember a quote by the famous doctor himself that goes: "Everybody lies; the only variable is about what."

So basically, what House is trying to say is that you may be able to tell when someone is lying, but can you tell what they're lying about, what they're covering up, or basically what the motivation behind the lie is?

In this chapter, we're going to talk about the motivations of people. Everybody is motivated by something. The feeling of hunger is your body giving you the motivation to want to eat so it can survive. It's basic human motivation. There are, of course, more complex motivations that we're going to get into. The thing is, if you want to be able to read a person's body language correctly, you need to be able to understand the motivations that drive them towards that end goal which is done by figuring out why someone is communicating in the way that they're communicating.

This doesn't just apply to lying. I just used the House quote to tie in the previous chapter. Everything everyone does is based around a motivation to try and get something to happen. When you ask someone on a date, you want to spend time with them or get to know them. This is fulfilling the need of socializing and developing relationships.

If you can identify the motive behind what someone is saying, you'll be able to highlight the truth behind their communications and why they're doing what they're doing. This is yet another strategy you can use to read people.

An easy way to think of this is to imagine you're driving on a highway. Every person is driving towards a destination which is their main motivation. If you're driving right alongside them, you might not be 100% sure of where they're going. However, if you take a good look at the car's movements, the blinkers, the position on the lane, the speed they approach the exits at, and so on, you should be able to make a close-to-accurate prediction of what they're doing and therefore adjust your own driving accordingly. Even if a person is lying to you, knowing what motivates them or what their *end game* is can help you figure out what the lie is all about and why they're doing what they do.

This one is going to be a little more difficult as it can get quite complicated, so bear with me as we go through this. Don't worry, we'll move slow and steady. Just so we're on the same page moving forward, I'll be defining *motives* as the conscious or unconscious moving factors for people's behaviors. Motives are the reasons we do what we do. *Behaviors* are the performances themselves or the actions that are reflective of a person's motivation. In other words, you feel the motive to eat, and your behavior is to get food from the fridge. Okay, let's get into it.

Maslow's Hierarchy of Needs

I remember first being introduced to motives and behaviors and this phrase came up and I thought to myself *Oh God, this is so complicated already. I'm in too deep!* Don't worry, it's not like that.

Maslow's Hierarchy of Needs is possibly one of the oldest rationales for understanding human motivation. It's not perfect, but what is? Maslow's Hierarchy of Needs is a lot like the Nutrition Pyramid. It explains that motives have a bottom-up approach. The bottom needs are the most basic and prevalent which must be met first before the other needs are addressed. There are five levels to basic human need, starting from the bottom, and these are:

- Physiological
- Safety
- Love/Belonging
- Esteem
- Self-Actualization

So, in the shape of a pyramid, physiological needs are on the bottom, aka, your basic human needs that need to be fulfilled, moving up to more spiritual needs. If it helps, you can easily find a visual diagram online. Here is a brief look at how these sections work and what they mean:

Physiological Needs

These are the main components that are aimed towards survival. According to Maslow's theory, humans are compelled to fulfill these needs first before they can ascend to higher levels. So, what exactly are these physiological needs? These are things like:

- Homeostasis, or the balance of the body in order to preserve its living condition
- Health
- Food
- Water
- Sleep
- Clothes
- Shelter

Notice how safety comes next. If you're fighting for your life after your plane goes down in the middle of the woods with no one around for miles, your first thoughts are going to be on survival. If you're starving and dehydrated, the chances are you're going to take risks to get food and water. Of course, we don't have this problem so much these days.

Safety Needs

After a person meets their basic physiological needs, the next step is their safety needs. Here are the typical considerations when it comes to safety needs:

- Personal security
- Emotional security
- Financial security
- Health and wellbeing
- Safety needs against accidents and illnesses

How do these things usually show themselves in an individual? You can see this by the way individuals purchase insurance policies, set up a retirement account, get jobs with security, open and maintain a savings account, and so on. Of course, you also have to consider people who are in war zones who are seeking out security in its most basic form: physical security. You will find that when in the midst of war, people seek security to maintain homeostasis or stay alive. The two stages are very much connected.

Social Belonging

Once you have the most basic needs and security, the next step is to seek out social belonging. You're surviving and your basic needs are met. Now it's time to bring other people into the equation.

We are social beings after all. It's hard-wired into us to connect with other people because fulfilling our basic needs is much easier when you're working together with other people. This need to be accepted by our peers is one of the most common driving forces for people. The need for social belonging is typically met by the following:

- Friendships
- Intimacy and romantic relationships
- Family

The need to be accepted in social groups is true regardless of the size of the group itself. This is why even when a person forms part of a small club in school, they still need to be part of the social circle within that club. Small social connections include family, friends, and colleagues in the typical workforce. You will notice that most people will go to extra lengths in order to have this sense of acceptance and belongingness in their chosen social circle. Failure to meet these needs leads to problems like social anxiety, clinical depression, and loneliness.

Self-Esteem

Fourth is self-esteem, which is somewhat connected to the third level. One thing you'll notice is that most people use the third level to jump to the fourth. Acceptance in their social circle tends to promote a person's self-esteem as they find themselves worthy because others find them worthy. What does this level cover? There are actually two versions of this: the lower and the higher version. The higher version speaks of self-esteem derived from others. There's a need for status, fame, prestige, recognition, and attention from others. This level is all about the ego.

The more difficult version is the higher one which speaks of self-esteem deriving from your own competency. This speaks of self-confidence, of knowing that you're capable of independence. This means being able to take care of yourself, knowing and fulfilling your own basic needs, and having the ability to meet those needs, perhaps even providing for the needs of others. This gives an individual a sense of value and prevents the possibility of having an inferiority complex.

Self-Actualization

This is the toughest level of the motivation pyramid and is all about managing to reach a person's full potential. Maslow describes it as the ability of an individual to accomplish everything they can possibly achieve in life. It is a lifetime goal and for many people, it can be difficult to pinpoint what that lifetime goal actually is. Others, however, know what this goal is but have a hard time reaching the lower levels, therefore making them unable to reach this pinnacle.

Self-actualization can include:

- Parenting
- Partner acquisition
- Utilizing and developing abilities

- Utilizing and developing talents
- Pursuing other goals
- Fulfilling your dreams

These self-actualization motives are described by Maslow as the intrinsic drive that pushes people forward into completion. People who have a clear grasp of this goal need to understand how their four needs in the pyramid interact with each other to help them achieve their ultimate goal.

The Sixth Level - Transcendence

I'm chucking this one in there just for interest purposes. Oddly enough, Maslow himself, creator of this hierarchy, has also talked about a sixth level. He called it Transcendence and according to him, it is a level of achievement where a person surrenders himself to something or someone more powerful than himself. You could call it God or surrendering yourself to the universe. While you may be thinking this is all about religion, that's not all there is to it. Transcendence is also pursued through meditative exercises. According to Maslow, transcendence refers to the highest and most holistic level of human consciousness.

I could write a whole book on this topic of transcendence, and trust me, I might. It's very interesting to read about and explore but would be hard to conceptualize as we look into motives, so I'm going to leave it for now. If you are interested, I recommend reading about Buddhist philosophy. It might surprise you.

Now I know what you're thinking. How does all this relate to reading people?

If you rely completely on Maslow's Hierarchy of Needs, you'll note that most people's actions are built towards reaching any of these five needs. It can be a tad difficult, but what you want to do is try to figure which of these five needs a person wants to achieve when confronted with a particular behavior. Is someone seeking social acceptance? Do they want to achieve the basic necessities of maintaining life? Do they want to have a sense of security? Are they trying to maintain a certain level of self-esteem? If you can figure out exactly what ultimate need someone is trying to fulfill, you can at least fill in the gaps and make a reading on what their body is saying.

When you're able to couple your ability to read body language and people's behaviors, as well as their motivations and directions, this is truly what it means to read somebody. Let's dive deep into this strategy.

Experience Matters when it comes to Motives

Unfortunately, there is a lot more to motivation than just figuring out which of the five needs a person wants to meet. The fact is that experience is a big predictor when it comes to figuring out motivations. Plus, it's on a case-by-case basis, with YOU as a big factor in the equation. Simply put—what does this person want from me? What need is this person trying to fulfill through me? What need can I fill for this person?

Are they feeling lonely and need someone to speak to? Are they trying to get you to do something? Are they trying to get information about someone or something else? Do they just need a friend? Figure out the motivation behind something someone says and you'll be able to understand what they're saying much more easily, thus, you're reading them.

Let's say you're ready to figure out people's motivations. You want to understand someone and help them fulfill their needs, to forge better connections. The question now is this: how do you start? The way you start varies from person to person, but there are certain *general rules* that can help you move forward with connections.

Here are some of the typical guidelines to make things easier for you:

Hidden Social Behaviors

We've been talking about the different actions of people and what they mean, but it's also important to look at the opposite end of the scale. You should keep in mind that more often than not, people draw in instead of pushing out. Many actions or reactions are done in order to suppress rather than express. For example, people close their arms, suck in their lips, or look away from people when withdrawing from an interaction and trying to hide. It's a pull motion, rather than a push.

How does this apply when you're trying to connect with people?

Well, you have to pay extra attention. There's this precise moment between a push and a pull when a person starts to react about something and then quickly holds that back in because they realize that they're showing emotions and feelings they don't want people to see. That's the moment you have to watch out for looking at people. Yes, this takes practice, but the more you try and notice, the better at noticing you'll be.

While you might not always catch this deliberate inaction, knowing that it's there is half the battle. More importantly, this should tell you that a lot of things are beneath the surface. This is why you need to focus on empathy, delving deep into the surface instead of just interpreting what people say without applying empathy.

Put yourself in the person's shoes and you should be able to at least have an idea of what they're trying to do or what they're trying to achieve. Allow me to give you an example for clarity.

You're at work. A project is due to be completed by the end of the week and it's Friday. You and your team realize that a large section of the project has been forgotten about and is missing. Everyone is trying to find who is responsible. People are stressed out and arguing amongst each other, and you suddenly realize that someone is about to speak and then stops themselves.

Using all the techniques we've spoken about throughout this book, it's pretty clear that you've just experienced the person who was supposed to do the work realize that they're supposed to do the work and have potentially gotten everyone else in trouble.

Notice how this person was about to say something but understands that they messed up, and now want to blend into the background, thus they remain silent. Their motive is to remain accepted by the group (social acceptance motives) and they don't want everyone to turn on them.

This is motives and hidden social behaviors in full effect. What do you do now that you have this information? You have a lot of options, but having empathy and compassion, you would perhaps choose to say it doesn't matter who forgot, what matters is pulling together and moving forward. Instead of pointing fingers, it's time to brainstorm solutions and explore your options.

When exploring solutions, you could perhaps pull up the person who withdrew to see what ideas they have and can bring to the table. Perhaps some of the work has already been done and wasn't finished on time. Either way, you're providing opportunities for redemption, once again (I would assume in a positive way) fulfilling this person's need of being socially accepted, and the problem is alleviated.

Of course, this is a simple example, but you can see how

the logic applies. You're looking for signs, reading everyone in the room, getting answers, identifying motives, and using this information to get things done.

Conceit trumps malice.

The next thing to keep in mind is that the vast majority of people aren't naturally evil, even if they may seem like it from time to time. If you're going to guess a person's motivation, malice should NOT be your first choice. In law, accused people are often considered *innocent until proven guilty* because the default setting is that a person is *good* unless there's enough evidence to show that they're not. This is also important if you want to understand people better. If you're heading into a conversation with someone and you're already thinking the worst of them, then your view is going to be biased and somewhat tainted.

An example of this that can be viewed from a lot of angles is imagining you're a shop owner and you've just caught someone stealing food. Immediately you're angry and you label this person as a criminal. Quite rightly too, they've been stealing from you.

However, when questioning their motivations, you try and figure out why. Are they young and just testing their limits? Are they old with no money? Are they a single mother with not enough money to feed their children? When you start bringing empathy into the equation, it can change everything and will create a very different conversation.

More often than not, people don't want to watch the world burn, but instead are acting through clouded emotions, acting out through past traumas, or are in a rough position.

In any situation where people are doing something that is harmful to others, first assume that they're doing it because they're unaware or ignorant or believe that their way is more important. By having this mindset, you are more likely to react in a kinder, more empathetic manner, which can be incredibly defusing to an intense situation and actually having a productive outcome.

The chances are you'd react by explaining to them exactly why their choice of action is not the best one. In contrast, walking into a situation believing a person is simply *evil* makes you react badly, perhaps even rudely or even violently, and that's not going to benefit anyone.

Selfish altruism often dictates behavior

Selfishness is often viewed as a desire to please only yourself while altruism is its exact opposite. Altruistic people are said to be selfless or want only the best for others. Oddly enough, people are driven by these two factors at the same time. Perhaps the simplest way to explain this is: people are giving, but they are giving in a way that also helps themselves. For example, people have no problem lending money to a friend, knowing that this particular friend can help them fix their computer or fix their car without charge. You trade in a car from a dealer and the two of you benefit. In some cases, helping someone is a sign that you have more power than that person, therefore helping you establish a feeling of dominance over another person.

When I was growing up, I lived in the country next to a charity farm. It was the kind of place where people with special needs would learn skills and kids could spend weekends outside. On paper, it's a good place, except the people running it seemed to be very much for show.

I'm not going to get into the politics of it, but a prime example that stuck with me for whatever reason was litter picking around the small town. The owners would do an annual litter pick up where they would publicize what they were doing and ensure that everyone understood that they were going out of their way to make the town a better place.

On the other hand, my father would go out and walk the dog every single morning and evening and would always come back with a small bag of litter chucked out the windows of drivers on the highway. Sure, he didn't walk all over the town and do it everywhere, only around our area, but he used to do it without any recognition from anyone else. If everyone in town had the same attitude, there would be no need for an annual litter pick up where everyone is doing it to make themselves feel as though they're doing some good.

Now, I'm not saying that any kind of litter pick up is wrong, or that the group activity is doing more harm than it is good. I use this example because it highlights how people will do good things sometimes because it benefits themselves and fulfills their own self-altruistic needs. Bear this in mind during your own interactions.

Memory is fickle

Another thing that might help you in understanding people for the better is that they don't have excellent memories. Memory is incredibly fickle for people and people are likely to forget certain things, ideas, or concepts.

I love the exercise of imagining you are holding a pen in your hand right now and then imagine dropping it. If you imagine hard enough, you can really convince yourself that you just dropped your pen. Weird, right? This is how bad human memories actually are. From experience, you'll think back to dropping your pen right now in a few weeks, and although you know it never happened, they'll still be a part of your memory that is trying to work out whether you did or not.

In the art of reading communication, if you're expecting someone to call or someone promised to do something for you, but they didn't, you can always assume it's because they simply forgot instead of deliberate malice. Hand in hand with the point above, do not go the route of assuming people are naturally evil as this will leave you feeling bitter and closed to the possibility of connecting and understanding others. Be loving and compassionate. This is how the best relationships are formed.

People are more emotional than they let on

Have you ever looked at someone being given surprising news and they seem to have very little reaction to it, even though the news is fairly shocking? That's because they're in shock and can't quite believe what they're being told, and even though they're feeling a ton of emotion, there are very few signs of it on the surface (apart from the silence and stunned look). The truth is that people are more emotional than they let on. If there's something seething beneath the surface, it's important to recognize that emotion even if you don't see it bubble out. It's perfectly normal for people to hold their feelings in. After all, outbursts are usually frowned upon in society and flamboyant enthusiasm is discouraged as being hyper or childish.

There is, of course, the taboo that men hold out and won't outwardly display their emotions as signs of being *weak*. These taboos are being challenged all the time, but they definitely still exist in many parts of the world. In other words, someone could be feeling really sad, but in an attempt to feel strong and in control, they are holding the feelings and emotions in, trying to bury them down as though they're not there whatsoever. In conversations and social interactions, you have to remember that people may not always be displaying their actual thoughts and emotions. Do not call people out on it unless you have to, but it's important to take it into consideration when interacting with them.

Unfortunately, the reverse of this holds true too. Unless you have made a full display of emotions or had a breakdown, people generally assume you're okay and act as if nothing has changed.

It can be quite frustrating if you're the one who's suppressing your emotions, but it feels perfectly fine for those at the other end. If you're on the opposite side of the situation (which means you're the one holding in your emotions), then do not take it personally. Don't *assume* that they *should* know your thoughts because people can only see as much as you allow them to see.

To round it all off, whenever you're interacting with someone, think about what kind of motives they have and what needs they are trying to fulfill.

Everybody, every single human on the planet, is driven by a motive and need of some kind and being able to highlight and understand what that is can take you such a long way in the journey of reading other people and their intentions.

This is one of the best ways you'll be able to read people. When you start understanding the motivations behind what's being said, you'll be able to see the true messages behind what they're trying to achieve and can see people for who they actually are, whether that's for better or for worse.

Chapter 8: Reading the Face and Body–Cues and What They Mean

Okay, we've covered a lot of topics in this book so far and we're looking at all kinds of communication, and as somewhat as a tease, we've covered how to read body language, but not directly. At this point, you'll have a few body language strategies under your belt, but usually for a purpose, such as identifying lies or motives. In this chapter, we're going to go hard and fast of actually reading people and their physical actions. This chapter is all about the very fundamentals of reading body language. Everything you've read up to this point has led to this.

Body language is a wide field and contrary to what you may think, it's not just the *body* per se, but also covers facial expressions, posture, gesture, eye movements, body movement, and even the lack of body movement itself. Body language is not unique to humans though; in fact, it's very obvious if you watch animals during their mating seasons. The dances and postures are hardly subtle as they do their best to attract the opposite sex.

But what about us humans? Body language in humans is far more complicated, however, so you'll have to be doubly observant. Unlike animals, there are lots of possible motivations that affect our body language. Even worse, some people make it a point of controlling their body's natural reaction or make sure that nothing shows through their body and facial expressions. Sometimes, they even fake those postures to give others the wrong impression. It's a minefield of infinite possibilities out there, but with the right foundations of knowledge, it's easily traversed.

The Science of Body Language

One thing you should note is that body language reading is not some difficult pseudoscience. It has been studied for years and has been solidified by legitimate studies. Today, the science of studying body language is called Kinesics and was founded by Ray Birdwhistell. It covers the following actions or conditions:

- Facial expressions
- Body posture
- Eye movement
- Use of space
- Touch
- Gestures

Throughout this chapter, we're going to explore each type of Kinesics, learning the foundations and basics of each so you know exactly what to look out for in your social interactions and what people mean through their non-verbal communications towards you. Sure, we've covered some of these already, but that's because everything in this book is intertwined with each other. Better yourself at these skills below, and you'll be able to read people, understand their motivations, connect with them as introverts or extroverts, and so on.

Facial Expressions

How good are you at reading facial expressions?

There are currently tests online that tell you whether you're good at reading facial expressions or not. In fact, some tests like Reading the Mind in the Eyes Test checks to see whether you can read a person's mind simply by looking at their eyes. If you're interested in taking the test yourself, check out the website: socialintelligence.labinthewild.org/mite. See how well you fare if you want. It's a lot of fun. I got 32 out of 36. Can you beat it? For purposes of improving communication, we're going to include all the elements that are included when it comes to reading facial expressions, which involves the eyes, eyebrows, lips, nose, and even the wrinkles around the eyes and mouth.

- Pupils – There is practically no way to fake the movement of the pupils when reading facial expressions. The pupils of the eye contract and expand without any sort of control on the part of a person. Typically, the pupils will expand when a person is interested and contract when they're not. Try this with a loved one. Say the name of a famous person they find attractive or a favorite food, and you can noticeably see the difference.

- Blinking Motion – The eyes typically blink six to ten times per minute. When a person looks at something they find interesting, however, that blinking rate slows down drastically. It's therefore a great indicator when someone finds something interesting or attractive. In fact, it's often used as a sign of flirting or interest in a romantic setting. In an office or social setting, unblinking eyes could be a signal that a person is very interested in what you have to say and listening and engaged with you throughout.

- Raising the head – Raising the head from a lowered position is a sign of captured interest. Think of a student who's looking down during an exam who suddenly raises their head when they hear something important. This is the kind of movement that we are trying to describe in this situation.

- Head tilt – A head tilt usually starts from a normal position of the head and then juts out at an angle. This is what makes it different from the motion of raising your head from a lowered position. A head tilt also indicates interest, usually towards the person or activity where it happens to be tilted towards. When combined with facial expressions like a narrowing of the eyebrows, it can be a sign of confusion, curiosity, questioning, or uncertainty. A head that's tilted backward may be a sign of suspicion.

Of course, let's not forget the typical head gestures that mean practically the same for everyone. These are:

- Nodding – usually signifies agreement
- Shaking the head – usually signifies disagreement

What's important about these gestures is that people are often conscious of doing this. Hence, gestures can be easily controlled by them depending on the situation. Some are able to stop the motion entirely while others turn it into very subtle gestures so that it would be very difficult to notice. However, more often than not, especially among most people going about their day-to-day lives, these are unconscious actions we all do.

Hands, Arms, and Gestures

- Shrug – A shrug is composed alongside a multitude of gestures which include exposed palms, hunched shoulders, and raised brows. It's a universal sign that indicates a lack of knowledge or uncertainty over a particular activity. It can often be translated as a sign that the other person doesn't know what you're saying or doesn't understand what you're trying to convey.

- Clenched Hands – Clenched hands are a sign of

repression. You're trying to prevent the burst of emotions like anger or frustration. It's a self-containment mechanism often used by people who don't want to do or say something out of order. In some cases, you can read this gesture as a sign that someone has a closed mind about what you're trying to say. In the alternative, open and relaxed hands are a sign of comfort and show a positive attitude with a mind welcome to new ideas.

- Hand Wringing – This is often interpreted as a sign of anxiety or nervousness. Playing with something in your hands also has the same interpretation.

- Handshake – You have to be careful with handshakes as this can say so much about a person and vice versa. I'm sure you've managed to have presumptions of people simply because of the way they shook your hand. The best handshake is often considered to be a firm, dry grip, that's quick but not too long. It shouldn't be too tight as to cause pain, but it should be strong enough to signify competence on the part of the person shaking their hand.

My advice is you practice your handshake with another person to help you decide on the best pressure to use when greeting someone this way. Note though—not all cultures accept handshakes as a viable way of greeting others. For example, people in India or those who practice the Muslim faith do not approve of handshakes as a way of greeting between men and women.

- Covering the mouth – Doing this is often shown as a sign of repression like a person who wanted to say something but decided against it at the last minute. Some people use this gesture as a way to show thinking or a thought process. A classic unconscious motion is pressing a thumb against a closed mouth, which indicates someone is actively holding back on what they want to say.

How to Apply this Knowledge

Simply noticing any of these actions can give you a clear indication of how the other person you're interacting with is feeling and will allow you the foundation to make a decision on how you want to proceed.

For example, if you say something and the other person clenches their fists or tightens their mouth, you know you may have overstepped a line and made the other person defensive. You can then choose to lighten the situation with a joke or clarify that no disrespect or malicious intent was meant, but instead, you meant something else, in which you would try to share your point of view from another perspective.

By ebbing and flowing in conversation this way, you're adapting how you communicate your messages, so they are best received by the people you're speaking to, thus nurturing the best possible relationships with these people, and have more chances of successfully getting what you want out of life.

Body Posture and Movement

You've probably noticed that reading body language involves paying attention to different parts of the body all at once. Some gestures are centered in just one area, like the face, and therefore are slightly easier than others. Some gestures, however, are scattered all over the body, which means that different parts are moving all at once. This makes it tougher to do a reading, but you'll find that with practice, the whole thing becomes easier.

Body posture and movement are big predictors of a person's thoughts and emotions. The general position of the chest, shoulders, legs, and so on will tell you if a person is aggressive, afraid, unsure, excited, and so on. Here are some of the typical changes in the body and what they indicate:

- A pumped-out chest is a sign of power, confidence, and dominance. Typically, when the chest is spread out, the shoulders are also stretched into a straight line, pushing the chest forward and making the person appear bigger. Combined with hands placed on the hips and this can be dubbed as the *Superman* pose which makes a person appear bigger and occupy more space. This is often seen as a sign of confidence and dominance. If you'll notice, many animals in the wild, when protecting their territory or trying to attract a mate, tend to make their bodies appear bigger so that they'll be easily noticed. Men and women do the same thing and often for the same reasons. What's more, the heart space is in the middle of the chest, making it a vulnerable area. To pump out your chest is to expose this space means that you're not afraid of anything in the given situation.

- Touching the chest can also be a sign of sincerity. You'll notice how people do this when they're trying to apologize or communicate how bad they feel or their condolences to another person. Again, this indicates the heart, meaning you're sharing this emotion you're feeling from the heart.

- Scratching or touching the chest can also be a sign of discomfort. Any kind of twitch along these lines can signify an uncomfortable feeling. Another point along these lines is when someone strokes their arms or shoulders. This is a self-soothing motion which also highlights a feeling of discomfort or uncertainty.

Just like the face gestures section, once you've identified a tell, it's important to make sure you're adapting your conversation style to follow suit, which is the best way to ensure you're being well received. Highlight cues in a person and keep the conversation moving forward.

Breathing

Breathing can tell you a lot about what a person feels.

You've probably noticed this already, not just in other people, but also in yourself. For example, you might hold your breath when excited or take short and shallow breaths when scared. Ever find yourself in a situation where it feels like you've forgotten to breathe or haven't breathed in a long time? That's what we're talking about here. Typically, deep and even breaths are indicative of relaxation, such as when you're sleeping or when you're sitting down watching a relaxing movie.

Excessive or shallow breathing, or holding your breath entirely, on the other hand, can be a sign of emotional turmoil. According to experts, mirroring a person's breathing pattern can also help forge a connection of mutual understanding between the two of you. Being able to match someone's breathing pattern essentially allows you to create a sense of normalcy in the situation, thereby guiding them into a sense of relaxation. Of course, this takes some skill to do, especially if the situation is nerve-wracking or intense. This comes back to having the ability to stay calm, balanced, and focused, without allowing your emotions to take you over. At the very least, being able to identify nervous breathing patterns can help you adjust your stance to make the other person feel comfortable—all without a word said to each other.

Proxemics

An excellent non-verbal way of communication is proxemics, which is the measurable distance between people. Basically, it characterizes relationships between people depending on their preferred distance in given situations. People often have personal space or a perceived territory that they're uncomfortable sharing with others. Think of this in a social setting. Would you feel comfortable if someone you met for the first time stands just mere inches away from you? Of course not! But if you're with your spouse or partner, you have no problem holding hands or putting your arms around each other. This is exactly what proxemics looks into and fortunately, the developer (Edward T. Hall) has done the research. He managed to write down the specifics of proximity and what they often indicate about relationships between people. Note that this proximity usually refers to men as women usually have a different idea of what the proper distance is in different situations:

Intimate Distance

This covers situations of touching, embracing, or even whispering

- Close – less than 6 inches
- Far – 6 to 18 inches

This is the type of distance you'll have with people you are intimate with. In the sense of reading other people, people who are this close to each other will typically be people who are close and have a tight relationship with each other. However, you may find yourself in a position where someone is in this distance and the rest of the body language is telling you that one person is not comfortable with the situation, allowing you the opportunity to step in and provide help if required.

Personal Distance

This typically involves interactions between family members or good friends

- Close – 1.5 to 2.5 feet
- Far – 2.5 to 4 feet

This is typically the distance you'll be when hanging out with people you know. If people are spending time this close to you, it means they trust you and feel comfortable with you.

Social Distance

This is the typical distance between acquaintances, and we're not just talking about COVID-19 requirements. This is perhaps the distance you would typically stand when talking to someone you've just met.

- Close – 4 to 7 feet

- Far – 7 to 12 feet

Public Distance

This is the distance used for public speaking purposes and would be used when addressing a crowd of people.

- Close – 12 to 25 feet
- Far – 25 feet or more

It's also important to note that distance can affect the posture or gestures of people. This is because there are instances when people don't have a say in the distance they have with others. For example, if you're in a cramped elevator or in a commercial airline, you do not exactly have the option of moving your body farther away from another person. In these instances, the rest of the body compensates by taking on some other form or angle relative to their position. This is why people in a cramped elevator tend to focus on their phones or look in any other direction aside from the person they're next to. It's a distraction from the uncomfortable feelings of being too close to someone they don't know. However, if someone's body language tells you that they're feeling confident and not uncomfortable by the presence of other people, even in traditionally awkward situations, it says a lot about this person.

An example of this would be in a job interview meeting. For example, a group of people is all riding an elevator up to a meeting, and you are one of three candidates for a job. One person is shy and in the corner, distracting themselves on their phone, you know they are nervous. If the other person is standing in the middle of the elevator and gives off the impression they're confident, you know they are perhaps well-prepared for the meeting and the person who will be the most competition to you for the job role.

In the alternative, people who are in an intimate relationship, or would like to be in an intimate relationship, tend to sit close to each other often.

Remember what we said about culture in a previous chapter, though? Acceptable proximity varies from culture to culture. For example, touching cheeks with each other can be a typical greeting in some countries while in others it is reserved for close family and friends.

Oculesics

This is actually known as a subcategory of body language. It focuses primarily on the movement of the eye, gazes, and other eye-centric movements that can help indicate what a person is thinking or feeling. Remember how people used to say the eyes are the windows to the soul? Well, there's a little bit of truth into it and with oculesics, you can have a bit more insight (pardon the pun!) on how the eyes can tell you what a person thinks or feels without a single word being said.

This body language technique is, again, limited by

culture, however, as eye gestures can change from one country to the next. For example, Latinos view extended eye contact as a sign of aggression while in some cases, it can show an interest in an individual. Asians see eye contact as anger while with Anglo-Saxons, the gesture could mean that they are telling the truth. Couple this with everything we spoke about in the previous chapter!

Haptics

Haptics is a non-verbal communication style that deals primarily with touching. Touching or skin-to-skin contact is perhaps the very first way people communicate. Parents communicate or connect with their babies through touch via different gestures. In fact, according to the Body Language Project, touching is the most developed sense at birth. In day-to-day life, touching includes handshakes, pats on the back, ruffles of the hair, brushes of the cheek, and so on. It signifies communication at different levels, managing to showcase all kinds of emotions from excitement, happiness, anger, devastation, and disappointment.

Haptics currently has five categories of communication by touch:

- *Functional or Professional.* This one is pretty self-explanatory. Basically, it refers to touch made in an office setting. One thing you have to remember in the office, however, is that touching is rarely encouraged. While at work, you're expected to maintain formal relationships, which means that skin-to-skin contact is not well-received. So, when is touching okay? Usually, touching gestures in the workplace are indicative of close friendship or sometimes *congratulations* for a job well done. It's a way of acknowledging that someone did well in their workplace, the gesture often encompassing a slap on the back, a handshake, or a simple squeezing motion of the shoulders. If you agree on the terms of a contract, you may shake hands that says: *yes, we're both happy and are in agreement,* so now we're allowing physical contact to prove this.

- *Friendship or Warmth.* This doesn't really necessitate explanation because friendly gestures may vary from one person to the next. Stereotypically, women will hug one another while men tend to have an energetic hug followed by a controlled slap on the back or an exaggerated handshake or fist bump. Some people do some air kisses; others do a complicated handshake routine, while others happily hug it out.

  Either way, any kind of friendly touch is a sign that the other person is trusted and allowed within someone's inner circle. You can use this in your own interactions by initiating handshakes if someone is feeling left out or isolated because you're telling them that everything is okay and you're allowing them into your inner circle.

- *Love or Intimacy.* This is all about emotional attachment and is usually displayed between romantic partners. They are public gestures that indicate that a person is *taken*. You've probably seen this through hand-holding, an arm around the shoulders, or placing hands on the hips.

- *Sexual or Arousal.* This one's a tad different from intimacy because this has sex for its motivation. During these touches, the intent is to have sexual relations, or perhaps they are right after one. It is often done in private, although the extent of a public display depends primarily on the culture of the people displaying it.

Bringing it All Together

There are two ways you can use this information. Don't worry, you don't need to remember it all and imprint every detail of what you've just read; the key is to be aware of what kinds of touch and gestures exist and then make decisions accordingly.

Let's say you walk into a business meeting. You can tell, just by how people are standing around each other and how close they are, who in the room is surrounded by friends, and which people aren't very connected, just based on physical space alone.

If you meet a group of friends and there's a couple in your group and they are physically keeping their distance more than you would expect, you'll have read the situation that something might not be right, such as they may have had an argument or falling out. You can then choose to distract the rest of the group or provide support. It's your call to decide.

Say your partner comes home from work and is being physically close with you. This means they are wanting to spend time with you, be intimate with you, and be in your company.

The point is, it doesn't matter what situation you're in, what you're doing by reading people is gathering the information that gives you a better stance at communicating effectively. Instead of mindlessly going into a situation and hoping for the best, you're actively looking for ways to relate to people in ways that will resonate with them in that moment of time. This is what it means to communicate effectively.

Chapter 9: Verbal Cues – Reading Between the Lines

Like it or not, most communication nowadays is done through words in a way that it has never been before— either written or oral. With the rise of the internet, written communication through email or chat messages is becoming the norm which means that your ability to read people shouldn't be limited to just face-to-face conversations.

In this chapter, we're going to do our best to decipher what people are really saying behind their words. Often dubbed as *reading between the lines* or *reading the room*, it's important to make a distinction between what people SAY and what they MEAN.

A word of caution before we go any further: you should know that there are people who mean exactly what they say. Take a good look at the MBTI we talked about in a previous chapter. The NT types are usually the ones who will tell you exactly what they want, and it would be in the most literal way possible—although, of course, this may vary depending on the situation and the unique style of the person. In these instances, I want you to follow a rule in law: when the words are clear you interpret them as straightforward and apply them accordingly. Only when words are ambiguous and vague should you consider the other cues in deciphering exactly what a person is trying to say.

Let's explore some of the best strategies when it comes to learning how to read between the lines.

Being a Better Listener

The first step in learning how to read between the lines is first listening with as much attention as you can muster. Remember, there is a big difference between listening and hearing. When listening, your main goal should be to learn new information. Don't be one of those people who simply listen in order to be polite to the person talking. Many psychologists will state that there are two types of listening. There is listening to learn and listening to respond.

I'm sure you know people in your life who you feel never listen to you but are rather waiting for you to finish talking so they can share their thoughts and opinions, not actually conversing with you in a proper conversation. This is not a nice way to be and won't win you any friends.

Instead, aim to find out something or glean information from them. You need to be curious about what the other person is saying; otherwise, you won't really absorb anything. Here's a test: if you walked out of a conversation without learning anything new, then you weren't really listening.

How do you become a better listener? Here are some tips:

Ask More Questions

Asking questions tells a person that you are interested and listening to the words they say. More importantly, questions allow you to clarify the situation, making it easier for you to forge connections between the information being given. This makes it possible for you to simplify the image in your head, arrive at accurate conclusions, and practice empathy or sympathy. Whatever the case may be, asking questions allows other people to elaborate and explain their position. More importantly, it encourages truthfulness in people because they feel compelled to tell you the unvarnished truth as recognition of the attention you are actually giving them.

Practice Active Listening

This is a technique that's been used for years and can help you really understand and create a story in your head. According to the director of the Center for Leadership at Northwestern University, active listening can be as simple as repeating back key words of what the speaker just said. It's like a little verbal nod of acknowledgment that says you're on the same page. The fact is that there are lots of opportunities to misunderstand what someone is saying. Active listening or giving a recap of what the other person said tells them that you're on the same page. Or if you aren't, it lets them correct any misconceptions you might have about the situation.

Wait Before Responding

Except for the instances when you need clarification, it's important to stay quiet until the speaker is finished. It's a typical rule in debates, meetings, and conversations, but you'll be surprised at how often people fail to follow this basic rule. The fact is that people can be so impatient that they don't even bother listening to a proposal completely before deciding to voice their thoughts, opinions, arguments, or even agreements. Remember what we said about listening to learn and listening to respond. This can be frustrating for the speaker and makes it impossible for you to fully absorb all the ideas at once. Also note that every interruption can distort the message the person is trying to convey, therefore making it more difficult for them to explain their standpoint.

Take Note of the Tone

As previously mentioned, the tone of voice can convey so much about a person. A low voice adds a sense of authority, a high-pitched one conveys nervousness, stammering can indicate doubt, and fast-paced words can indicate anxiety. Also, paying attention to which words are given emphasis can change how the sentence is perceived. For example, they may be putting emphasis on the word *maybe* or perhaps they stuttered the word *yes* as a reply. This could be indicative that although they want to say *no*, they're put in the position where they feel as though they can't refuse.

Taking Action: Aligning Body Language with Verbal Cues

Let's say you're in a conversation with someone and you're piecing together everything we've been learning about so far. You're reading their body language and picking up on physical cues, and you're listening to what they're saying properly and picking up on their verbal cues. How do you piece the two together to get an accurate image of what someone is saying, therefore providing you with the foundation of knowledge that allows you to communicate back most effectively?

First, start with the basics. Are the physical and verbal cues you're receiving in alignment? For a running example, we're going to say you're in a job interview for your dream job, and you're obviously hoping to make a good impression.

You're talking to the recruiter. Their body language is open and positive. You feel welcomed and things are going well. The verbal cues are also positive. The recruiter is saying positive things and saying you're doing well, and you'd make a great fit at the company. That's excellent. Keep doing what you're doing.

On the other hand, what if the cues aren't aligned? Let's say you're being told *this is good. That's excellent.* But what if the recruiter is closed off, there's a lack of eye contact, and you're not being paid much attention?

You're reading the situation and you're reading that the recruiter is not on the same wavelength as you.

What do you do?

Well, you use what you've learned to turn the situation around. What body language do you read? If the recruiter is closed off and slumped, are they bored or having a bad day? If shoulders are raised and they are clearly experiencing stress, this could be the case. Now you can decide whether to carry on or connect with the recruiter. You could say something like;

"Just out of curiosity, do you think it's incredibly stressful to work here? Should I be prepared for the worst?"

To which they reply:

"Well, you know how it is. There are good days and bad days. I'm just due for a day off."

"You know, if I did end up here, I'd be more than happy to advocate with you for more days off during the week. We could set up a picket fence and everything."

Obviously, you're just joking, but what you've done is change the situation entirely. Instead of just being another candidate that sat in front of the recruiter who's having a bad day, you've made the situation personal. You've connected with the recruiter and lightened the situation. You're not just here for the job, but you're actually a people person who talks to other people like they are people, not just holding the image that you're dealing with a faceless business.

Guess who's going to stand out in the recruiter's mind now? I'm not saying you need to dive into the situation and give the recruiter a space to talk about all their problems. That's not professional. What you are doing, however, is reading the situation, identifying the problems, and taking action to communicate as effectively as possible.

It all starts with reading and being aware of the situation. Then choose to react. If you're in a group interview with another candidate, you'll want to use your knowledge of body language to make yourself come across as confident and as though you're supposed to be where you are.

If you get onto a topic of conversation where the other candidate shrinks away and becomes quiet, you know this is going to be a topic that might be their downfall and can run off of this. On the other hand, if the recruiter is energetic and placing special interest in a certain topic, then you know this is going to be an important area of business that the company is looking into, so you know the section you're heading into may require more care and attention with your approach.

Of course, we could go into situations and examples until the cows come home, but the main takeaway I want you to think about is how you can actionably use the information you're learning in your day-to-day interactions. Through trial, error, and experience, you'll see dramatic results.

Chapter 10: The Art of Thin-Slicing

Time and again, I talked about the importance of practice and experience in this book. I placed emphasis on the fact that you need to know a person, or at the very least, be able to establish a baseline before making readings or arriving at conclusions about a specific individual. Making assumptions is probably going to leave you in a worse place than if you didn't try these techniques at all.

You're probably asking: but what if I don't know the person for a long time before trying these techniques? What if I never have the chance to actually know them? So far in this book, I still haven't discussed the possibility of *speed-reading* people through non-verbal communication. There will be instances when you don't have the luxury of time. You will need to make a snap-second decision in a particular situation based only on non-verbal cues. What do you do then?

Let me introduce to you the concept of thin-slicing. This is a concept that's been talked about by various authors, including the best-selling writer, Malcolm Gladwell in his book: Blink.

What Is Thin-Slicing?

Thin-slicing is a *reading* technique that needs only a short span of time for reading. It's a term used in psychology that describes a person's ability to find patterns and make conclusions based only on very small factors or narrow windows of exposure—hence the thin slices. The beauty here is that even with such thinly sliced information, you can still get accurate results as if you've observed this person for a long period of time.

How Thin-Slicing Translates to Day-to-Day Life

In Gladwell's book *Blink*, he talks about how art connoisseurs often know when a particular work of art is the real thing or just the copy of an original. In that split second that they see something, even before all the scientific tests are done, they can say when a work does not deserve all the accolades given to it. A good example would be the Getty Kouros, which was sold for 10 million dollars and was verified by scientists to be from around 530 B.C. However, many art scholars look at it and see a modern forgery, which means that it's not worth the 10 million dollars that were used to buy it. How do they do it? What are the tells that give it away? What are the scholars looking for?

This split-second ability of art scholars to identify what's fake and what's not is the very context of thin slicing. Believe it or not, we also do this in day-to-day life, you just might not realize it yet. Here are some situations when thin-slicing has been proven to be effective.

First Impressions

Have you ever listened to a lecture for five minutes and could instantly tell if the lecturer is a good one or not? Studies show that students listening to a five-minute lecture are capable of judging whether a professor is good or not, in the same way as a student who has had that same professor for the whole semester.

Sexual Preferences

A study conducted in 1999 showed that people can perceive a person's sexual orientation accurately. Based only on silent videos spanning 10 seconds, people had an accuracy rate of 70% when perceiving a person's gender preference or sexual orientation. This goes back to using your gut instinct to read someone. While you can't be completely sure, using this information coupled with reading verbal and non-verbal cues is essential when accurately reading someone.

Detecting Lies

Okay, so I dedicated a whole chapter to this, so it doesn't really bear repeating. Let's just say that most people have a gut feeling when they're being lied to. Perhaps one of the most powerful examples of thin-slicing lies is when it comes to relationships. People in relationships sometimes say they *feel* as though their partner is being dishonest, but perhaps can't seem to prove why they feel this way.

A study conducted by the University of Texas at El Paso once tested the theory of thin slicing by asking one group to provide a verbal rationale for why they did something.

It turns out that the group asked to rationalize their decisions performed more poorly than the group asked to just make their decisions instantaneously using gut instinct.

What does this tell us?

It says that when confronted with rationalized thinking, logic is not always the best approach and that our gut instinct can be more accurate. Again, if you get a feeling about someone while reading them, don't take it as 100% truth, but instead, be exact with using this information when trying to get an accurate image of what a person is communicating to you.

Parent Interactions

One interesting aspect of thin-slicing where it becomes prominent is the interaction of parents with their children. According to research, a parent's tone of voice when addressing a normal child and one with a behavioral problem have a slight variation that's obvious enough to be noted by teachers.

This is crucial in educational settings as teachers meet parents on the first day of class usually. By simply watching parent-child interactions, teachers can already tell if they have to pay more attention to the child for behavioral issues, or if they can relax more knowing that the child will probably behave. Simply through teacher-student interaction, observers can tell which teachers are biased and which teachers have unrealistic expectations over their charges.

These are just a handful of ways that thin slicing can appear in your day-to-day life. You're basically reading situations quickly using your instincts and a bit of background knowledge that you've learned throughout this book. Now, let's start honing these abilities even further.

The Basics of Thin-Slicing

Here's a question: what's the element we're looking at when it comes to thin-slicing?

When you're thin-slicing, you're looking at a small portion of information to judge a whole. But what information are we really looking at? What's the important information to look at to make an accurate reading, and what information is best left to the side?

Imagine you're speed dating. What particular factor do you look at in deciding whether you want to see someone else again? What is the heaviest element that decides the case?

As much as I want to answer this question, the fact is that it varies from one situation to the next, and it varies depending on the person you are. If you're speed dating because you want to hook up with someone for the night, you're going to be looking for different things than someone looking for a long-term relationship. My question is, how do you determine who is on the lookout for what, allowing you to spend your efforts in the right places? Of course, I'm talking about in all aspects of your life, not just in a speed dating concept! In an effort to answer this question, however, let me give you an example.

In Malcom Gladwell's book, he talks about thin-slicing marriages. Within seconds of seeing a couple, Gladwell claims it's possible to accurately tell if it will result in a divorce or not. How?

Accordingly, this one element is: contempt. Marriages that seem to be doomed to fail involve those where one partner seems to be contemptuous or resentful of another. This means that one person in a couple feels superior over the other and interacts with them in a way that makes the other person feel less of a person. Contempt can be seen through some of the interactions between these couples, which leads to a conclusion that they're not bound to last.

So, is this true for all thin-slices? Can you just focus on ONE element and already make an accurate prediction of a specific situation? Studies show that you can, but again, the accuracy is not as reliable as when you rely on big slices of information.

How Do You Thin-Slice?

Okay, let's get to the core of it. How do you accurately

thin slice? Remember, you're really only going to be thin-slicing people you don't have a baseline for, so let's say you've rolled up to a business and you're about to try to sell a product.

Let's go.

First, take note of the person's appearance. Are they dressed for the meeting? Do they look professional, like they pride themselves on their work, or do they look disinterested? If it's the latter, they might not be interested at all, so you can decide whether you're wasting your time or you want to take a different, more engaging approach.

This continues with how much attention they are paying you. Are they engaged? If someone says they're not interested in paying such a high price for your product, but they're engaged with what you're saying, then you know that the price isn't so much of a turn off because they still want or need what you have to offer. If the price was too high and they weren't engaged, they would simply tell you they're not interested.

Remember to go with your gut feelings. If you apply too much logic and overthink reading someone, you can provide yourself with false information. If you feel like the person is bored, then start engaging with them more, make your presentation more exciting, or get more personal. Draw the other person into what you're saying. Act on impulse. When you know what you're looking for, less is more.

Finally, go off the situation you're in. In a business setting, there are typically a few personal cues you'll be picking up on. However, on a date, you'll be looking for intimate cues, such as eye contact, touch, and physical proximity. The context of things you're looking for changes depending on the situation you're in. You should hopefully have more of an idea of what to look for here as you've made your way through this book.

Chapter 11: What About Me?

So far in this book, we talked about other people. Specifically, about the different personality types, how to identify a personality type, how to read body language, and so on. Really, the only thing we haven't talked about is you. When it comes right down to it, YOU are the most important part of the equation.

Why is this? I'd like to remind you that this book's ultimate goal is to help you *connect* with people, and not all connections are equal. The way you connect with a work friend is very different from the way you connect with a school friend or a neighbor.

Would you tell a work friend in-depth information about yourself in the same way you'd tell a high school friend or your best friend? Of course not!

Of course, that's not the only factor at play here. The way you communicate is also dictated by the type of person you are. All the personality types and traits we discussed in a previous chapter apply to you too! Hence, you have to figure out if you're an introvert or extrovert, an intuitive or a sensor, a thinker or a feeler, and a perceiver or judger.

To effectively communicate with someone, you can't just read the other person and hope for the best, because they're unconsciously, or even consciously, going to be reading you too. This means you need to be in control of how you communicate and present yourself in the most effective way, depending on the situation you're in and who you're talking to.

Understanding the Importance of You

Your ability to connect with people is limited by your own personality. For example, if you're an extrovert, how are you supposed to connect with someone who is an introvert? If you're a feeler, how do you make connections with someone who is a sensor? This is why I strongly encourage you to take the Myers Briggs test I wrote about earlier and learn as much about yourself as possible.

This is crucial because if you *really* want to make that connection, you might find yourself in situations that you're uncomfortable in.

What is your personality type?

I want you to be aware of your own strengths and shortcomings when it comes to connecting and communicating with people, which is another reason why I recommend the Myers Briggs test. Once you learn about who you are, whether you're introverted and extroverted and so on, you can then play to your strengths and address your weaknesses.

You might be an introvert trying to connect with an extrovert which makes the job doubly hard for you. Perhaps the situation is vice versa. By realizing your personality type, you should be able to make headway and figure out what factors are holding you back from reaching your communication goals.

What is my communication style?

Now that you're learning about yourself, we have to talk about the kind of communicator you happen to be. You might not realize it, but you have a specific way of communicating, just like everyone else does. The goal is to adjust your communication style slightly so that you can easily connect with others through verbal and non-verbal means.

Here are the typical communication styles today. Keep in mind that these communication styles apply to others as well as to you.

Analytical Communicator

The analytical communicator makes good use of data and real numbers. If this is you, then you like to use references when establishing your point. If this is you, then this is probably your biggest drawback as you are likely to become silent during emotional conversations, having problems putting what you think or feel into words.

If you prefer this type of communication, keep in mind that you may sound completely cold or unfeeling. People are going to feel unsure about making emotional gestures towards you because they think you're going to react badly to them. You have to learn how to be a bit softer or open up to others in order to encourage discourse.

Intuitive

Intuitive communicators are the kinds who like to see the big picture. They like to start with the general rule and then whittle it down to the basics. They are really not fond of the details but prefer a big view or a bird's-eye view of what's going on.

What adjustment could you make as an intuitive? You could perhaps make an effort towards explaining your thought process. Give others the time to follow your idea, making sure that each point has been explained before arriving at the conclusion. Try to develop a bit more patience because not everyone prefers your quick method of communication.

Functional

Functional communicators are the types who like to itemize steps from Point A to Point Z. Basically they are the opposite of an intuitive communicator. They like the step-by-step fashion, making sure that nothing gets missed.

An important thing to remember as a functional communicator is to improve your skills in grabbing and maintaining the attention of your audience. The small details leading towards a bigger end can be quite taxing for people and they will quickly lose interest during a representation. Hence, you can make use of body language techniques to encourage interest and guarantee that people are on the same page as you.

Personal Communicator

Finally, we have the personal communicator who prefers to focus on the emotional aspect of things. You find it important to figure out not just what a person is thinking but also what they feel about a particular situation.

The downside of this is that personal communicators can be easily affected by the underlying emotional atmosphere. If overwhelmed, you might find yourself acting out instead of being the glue that keeps the group sane. Hence, as a personal communicator, your best adjustment would be to keep a rational and level head in order to keep everyone within acceptable ranges of communication.

One thing I want you to understand is that there is no *best* communication style. All these styles have a specific advantage, depending on the use. It's therefore important to be flexible with your communication style so that you'll be able to adjust to the situation. Remember, this is all about preferences so you might actually find yourself able to switch from one communication style to the next. The more you practice these techniques, the better you become in taking on any role that's needed in that particular situation.

The Checklist of Body Language

When talking to someone, it's crucial that you're aware of how you're presenting yourself and the message that you're unconsciously sending out to others. Bear things in mind like:

Signs of Negative Body Language

- Arms folded in front of the body
- Tense or minimal facial expression
- Body turned away from another person
- Downcast eyes
- A lack of eye contact

Disengaged Body Language

- Bad sitting posture
- Writing or doodling
- Gazing or staring off into space
- Downcast head
- Fidgeting or fiddling with an item

Of course, you might want to act this way to send a certain message. If, however, you want to keep things positive, you'll need to switch things up.

Positive Body Language

- Have an open posture
- Keep the muscles relaxed without slouching on the chair
- Keep your body upright and hands placed on the side or comfortably folded in front of you.
- Avoid touching your face when talking to another person.
- Maintain eye contact.
- Use a firm handshake.

Practicing at Home

Before you head out into the world and start practicing some of these techniques yourself, try honing them in front of the mirror at home and see for yourself how much of a difference it can make in your confidence, and your ability to portray yourself to others.

Here are some tips on things to try.

Maintain a positive posture.

Stand or sit upright with your shoulders and arms at your sides. You can fold your hands in front of you or keep them relaxed at your sides. You can also use hand gestures to emphasize what you're trying to say. Whatever you do, do NOT slouch or put those hands in your pockets, as this would make you look like you're not interested in the situation.

Make use of open hand gestures.

Open hand gestures invite the audience to listen and give off positive vibes. If you can't keep your hands relaxed at your sides, then position them so that the upper arms are close to your body and the palms are facing up. This communicates a willingness to communicate on a deeper level.

Mastering Your Voice

Have you ever tried hearing yourself speak in front of a mirror? Don't worry, it doesn't mean you're crazy to talk to yourself, especially in the context of practicing to become a more effective communicator.

Try talking as though you're having a conversation with someone and see how changing your tone of voice can make such a big difference to what you're saying. Again, practice makes perfect, so experiment and see what works for you.

Don't Forget the Golden Rule!

Remember, the whole point of this book is to help you *connect* with people, so I need you to understand that the Golden Rule still applies here. What's that?

It simply states: Do unto others what you would have them do unto you.

Hence, if you want to connect with people and forge stronger relationships with them, you'll have to keep their wants and needs in mind. If you find yourself getting mixed signals or unsure about how to go forward, just ask yourself, *Would I want this for me?* If you don't want the same thing to be done to you, then it makes sense that others don't want it to be done to them either!

Mastering Intermediate Body Language Techniques

Once you've mastered the basics of controlling how you communicate, you can start implementing more advanced strategies to help you achieve even better results. These can seem a little weird or maybe even forced at first, but they can make such a big difference in the way you're perceived and connect with others. However, you can start implementing these in your own time.

Use mirroring.

You've probably heard about this often, which is only because it works so well. Mirroring is a technique where you subtly mirror or copy the body language of the person you're talking to. This has the effect of building rapport, as mirroring makes it look like the two of you are on the same page.

It is important to note though mirroring is a fairly well-known technique nowadays so there's a chance the other person also knows you're doing it. Therefore, it's important not to copy every single gesture they make, as this will have the opposite effect.

Put emphasis on the gestures that show interest.

Do not overdo it, but make a point of nodding, smiling, and keeping your body relaxed during an interview. The technique of slightly leaning in towards the other person can also work, allowing you to create the image of rapport.

If you're ever asked a difficult question, don't be afraid to pause and think about what you're going to say first. Touch your cheek, gaze off a little, or bite your lips. This will show the other person that you're reflecting on your answer or putting the proper amount of thought into it.

Chapter 12: Further Body Language Tips

Your ability to read the non-verbal communication of the people around you is one thing. Your ability to convey non-verbal messages on your own is another. Communication takes two things: the initial message and the reply. Simply put, I want you to be good with non-verbal communication as well, not just with the initial message but also with the reply. At the very least, I want you to be able to use body language to your advantage.

Here's a secret though: studies show that how you move or the body posture you assume also contributes to how you feel. It is not just a one-way street.

What does this mean?

For example, if you feel sad or down, you tend to slouch your body. When people see you doing this, they can instantly tell that you feel sad or are depressed. Your posture is a non-verbal sign of what you're feeling inside.

But the reverse actually holds true! This means that even if you feel bad but posture your body in a way that conveys confidence, you will slowly gain confidence. It's a mind over matter thing and it can help you through many problems in life, wiring your mind to deal with situations in different ways, and you actually have control over this as long as you're mindful!

How do you do this? Here are some body language tips to help you convey the exact message you want to make in any situation:

If You Want to Feel Confident

Ever seen the pose Superman makes? This is the *confidence* pose that could make you feel like you're more confident than usual. This high-power pose stimulates testosterone levels and lowers the amount of cortisol in the body. As you probably know, cortisol is a stress hormone and the less of this in your body, the better it would be for you. What's the pose exactly? Hands on your hips, feet apart, and your shoulders stretched wide with the chest puffed out.

Try not to overdo it too much so people don't look at you weirdly because there is such a thing as taking it too far. But this should work perfectly and give you the confidence boost you need for any given situation.

Of course, there are other confidence poses out there, verified by Harvard no less. It's the high-power pose of leaning back in your chair, hands on your head, and feet up on the desk. You've probably seen this being done by businessmen in movies when they want to show how confident they are. As it turns out, it works perfectly in boosting morale and ego. Of course, you can't do this while in a meeting, but if you're tackling a hard problem at the office, assuming this pose for a few seconds should help.

To Make People Participate, Look Like You Are Actually Listening

This might seem like a no-brainer, but a lot of people forget the value of listening when someone speaks. If you want to increase the participation in a meeting, verbal methods aren't enough. You have to *show* people that you're really listening to what they have to say. Look at people when they speak and nod along with them in order to create the sense of being listened to.

Don't doodle or tap on your phone or check the room to see what the others are doing. Instead, focus on the person speaking and establish eye contact. This will help encourage people into verbalizing their thoughts and create a more honest atmosphere for discourse.

Smile to Promote Good Feelings

A genuine smile stimulates not only your sense of well-being, but it likewise tells those around that you're cooperative, approachable, and trustworthy. A genuine smile comes on slowly, lights up the face, crinkles the eyes, and fades slowly away. Most importantly, smiling has a direct influence on how people respond to you. When you smile at somebody, they almost always will smile in return. That's just basic human psychology.

Since facial expressions elicit corresponding feelings, the smiles you get back actually change the person's emotional state positively.

Look at People's Feet for Added Insight

The feet are also a big deal when it comes to body language. Feet are tapped, played with, or pointed in different directions, depending on a person's mood. Perhaps one of the biggest indicators is where the feet are pointed.

If the foot is directed away from you during a conversation, then chances are that person doesn't really want to talk. If it is pointed towards you, however, then they're fully engaged in the conversation.

Keep Your Voice Low for an Authoritative Sound

Let your voice relax before making an important call or speech. It appears that a low and steady voice communicates authority and power as opposed to a high one. It's a very subtle way of affecting the senses, relaxing other people, and putting you in a position of power without trying too much.

Be Naturally You

Perhaps the most important consideration here is to make sure you're being yourself. With everything you've learned, it could be so easy to fall into the trap of just being a body language reading robot, but that seems stiff and unnatural. If you're forcing how you are and it comes across as fake, this is simply counter-productive to your efforts.

Be relaxed. Don't take things too seriously, and just be yourself!

Conclusion

So there we have it, we've arrived at the end of this book! I'm happy you have made it this far and I hope you found all the information stated here useful for day-to-day life. Practice makes perfect, so take everything you've learned and apply it. Even if it feels weird or unusual at first, experience will take you places and will help you build your confidence tenfold, allowing you to communicate most effectively during the times where it matters most.

You can nurture such beautiful, meaningful relationships with anybody in your life if you're able to communicate properly, which means both listening and speaking with purpose and accuracy.

I understand there's a lot to take in and a ton of information to learn, but don't worry. Even if things are a little bit confusing even at this stage—it's supposed to be. Humans aren't simple creatures, and our minds are infinitely complex. You're never going to understand everything, nor do you need to. The fact is that understanding people is a lifetime process so you will find the need to constantly evaluate your baselines as you move forward.

There's one thing I want you to remember when using this book: you only have control over your own values, actions, and reactions. It doesn't matter how badly you want to connect or forge ties with someone—you cannot *force* people to like you if their values are intrinsically different from yours.

Keep in mind that connection is based on similarities and there's no point connecting with someone when nothing is similar between the two of you. Remember, you matter first. Your values are personal to you and you should NOT allow other people to choose your values.

So, what do you do now? Here's what I want you to do:

1. I want you to take a good look at yourself and assess your values, personality, communication style, goals, and everything else that pertains to you. I want you to get to know yourself deeply first before attempting to know others.

2. Your next step would be to observe yourself. What are your mannerisms, your behavior, and your tendencies when confronted with specific situations? I want you to know exactly what you're doing wrong and what you're doing right.

3. Next is cultivating a system of thinking, analyzing, and discovering your values and motivations before pursuing a behavior. Even before you do something, I want you to pause and think about why you're doing it. What's your ultimate goal and what's the motivation behind it? Feel free to use Maslow's Hierarchy of Needs for this to help you further narrow down your own motivations.

4. Once you've figured out your goals and motivations, I want you to take a good look at the actions you propose to take. Are those actions in line with your goals and motivations? Will they achieve the results you want? What other roads are there for you to take to get the same results, but with much less hindrance on your part?

5. I encourage you to practice these four steps consistently to get to know yourself better through personal analysis. Only after you're comfortable understanding yourself, can you feel comfortable in understanding others. One thing I want you to remember though: you don't have to understand yourself 100%! Face it, people are a mystery and sometimes, we can be a mystery to ourselves too. All I encourage you to do is to try as often and as hard as you can to trace your motivations before pursuing any sort of significant action.

Let's say you're comfortable understanding your own motivations at this point—what about other people? Here's what I want you to do:

a) First, I discourage you against reading too much into people you don't know or barely know. While thin-slicing is highly effective, you should not use this as a way to figure out everything around you. People-watching can be fun and a good way to hone your skills, but don't take things too seriously.

b) Start by focusing only on a small group of people. Make decisions based on conscious *reading* efforts but keep it simple or in situations where getting it wrong wouldn't have negative consequences in your life. Remember, you're testing the waters here and honing your skills.

c) I want you to always keep in mind that this book was written to help you CONNECT with people through developed verbal and non-verbal skills. Hence, try not to use your new superpowers for evil and keep connections in mind when trying to decipher people. You're not trying to maliciously manipulate people into doing what you want. Of course, you have goals and needs to fulfill, but this is about communicating that effectively.

d) Develop a pattern when observing people. Routine is everything when it comes to learning a new skill. This means having a fairly good idea of where to start when attempting to understand them. For example, you look at the feet first, then the hands, then the face, or any other sequence you may choose. Having this pre-set programming on where to look gives you a story-type reading experience that can help with any conclusions you might have about the situation. The beauty here is that as you practice this technique, it becomes second nature to the point where you don't even have to consciously guide yourself through the process. Your mind instantly goes to these body parts in order to interpret what they mean.

e) Learn the art of listening and try not to be too self-absorbed. Even as an extrovert, you should be able to recognize the enjoyment of being able to sit back in one corner of the room and just take in the different movements and reactions of people as they interact with each other.

f) If you find things too difficult, I suggest you watch a movie multiple times and pay attention not just to the words but also to the actions and movements of the actors. Actors are trained in the proper action and reaction processes in different situations to make them look realistic. Their facial expressions and even the slightest movement of the hands can convey so much and can help hone your skills in prediction. It's by far the safest way of approaching body language understanding while enjoying yourself in the process. Make sure to watch movies with very good actors known for their excellent skills in the art. Meryl Streep movies are perhaps one of the best to do this, focusing primarily on the movement of this amazing actress.

g) The beauty of watching movies is that there's a way for you to confirm what you suspect about a certain situation. You can look at a person's expression in one scene and guess what they think or feel. In a later scene, these emotions are often expressed out loud or given further focus, therefore allowing you to figure out if what you initially thought was correct.

h) When reading people in the real world, observe and keep your conclusions to yourself. Do not go around telling people that you've *read* how a particular coworker acts and make expressive predictions because of it. I want you to keep any conclusions or ideas you have close to your heart and only use them when needed.

i) Practice, practice, practice! The beauty of reading body language is that you never run out of people to observe or body language to read. There's always an endless supply of them, so feel free to practice as often as you want. Note though that acting on those observations isn't always advisable. Think about it multiple times before actually making a decision.

Yes, you are capable of reading people and making connections simply by honing your verbal and non-verbal skills! But it takes time, patience, and drive. It might seem like a big project at first, but don't let this stop you! Unless you live under a rock, forging connections and communicating with others is an integral part of your life. You will find that by mastering this talent, you too can achieve the kind of success that only a few can boast about.

Thank you!

Before you go, I just wanted to say thank you for purchasing my book.

You could have picked from dozens of other books on the same topic, but you took a chance and chose this one.

So, a HUGE thanks to you for getting this book and for reading all the way to the end.

Now I wanted to ask you for a small favor. **Could you please consider posting a review on the platform? Reviews are one of the easiest ways to support the work of independent authors.**

This feedback will help me continue to write the type of books that will help you get the results you want. So if you enjoyed it, please let me know.

Also by James W. Williams

- Communication Skills Training: How to Talk to Anyone, Connect Effortlessly, Develop Charisma, and Become a People Person

- How to Make People Laugh: Develop Confidence and Charisma, Master Improv Comedy, and Be More Witty with Anyone, Anytime, Anywhere

- Digital Minimalism in Everyday Life: Overcome Technology Addiction, Declutter Your Mind, and Reclaim Your Freedom

- Self-discipline Mastery: Develop Navy Seal Mental Toughness, Unbreakable Grit, Spartan Mindset, Build Good Habits, and Increase Your Productivity

- How to Make People Like You: 19 Science-Based Methods to Increase Your Charisma, Spark Attraction, Win Friends, and Connect Effortlessly

- How to Make People Do What You Want: Methods of Subtle Psychology to Read People, Persuade, and Influence Human Behavior

- How to Talk to Anyone About Anything: Improve Your Social Skills, Master Small Talk, Connect Effortlessly, and Make Real Friends

- Listening Skills Training: How to Truly Listen, Understand, and Validate for Better and Deeper Connections

- How to Spot a Liar: A Practical Guide to Speed Read People, Decipher Body Language, Detect Deception, and Get to The Truth

- Easy Self-Discipline: How to Resist Temptations, Build Good Habits, and Achieve Your Goals WITHOUT Will Power or Mental Toughness

Resources

- The Difference Between Introverts And Extroverts, In 1 Simple Chart. (2019, May 28). Retrieved from https://www.huffpost.com/entry/difference-between-introverts-extroverts-chart_n_57f794c2e4b0b6a430316b3a

- What makes an extravert?. (2013, July 19). Retrieved from https://mindhacks.com/2013/07/22/what-makes-an-extravert/

- Kinesics. (2004, November 6). Retrieved from https://en.wikipedia.org/wiki/Kinesics

- Reading facial expressions of emotion. (n.d.). Retrieved from https://www.apa.org/science/about/psa/2011/05/facial-expressions

- A psychometric analysis of the reading the mind in the eyes test: toward a brief form for research and applied settings. (n.d.). Retrieved from https://www.ncbi.nlm.nih.gov/pmc/articles/PMC4593947/

- How to Tell An Introvert From An Extrovert. (2014, October 25). Retrieved from https://www.bustle.com/articles/45805-how-to-tell-an-introvert-from-an-extrovert-

- Body Language: Picking Up and Understanding Nonverbal Signals. (n.d.). Retrieved from https://www.mindtools.com/pages/article/Body_Language.htm

- How to Communicate Effectively with any Myers-Briggs® Personality Type. (2019, December 26). Retrieved from https://www.psychologyjunkie.com/2017/05/22/communicate-effectively-myers-briggs-personality-type/

- Cohen, S., Sherrod, D. R., & Clark, M. S. (1986). Social Skills and the Stress-Protective Role of Social Support. *Journal of Personality and Social Psychology*, 50(5), 963-973.

- Sirven, N., & Debrand, T. (2008). Social participation and healthy ageing: An international comparison using SHARE data. *Social Science & Medicine*, 67, 2017-2026.

- Steptoe, A., Dockray, S., & Wardle, J. (2009). Positive Affect and Psychobiological Processes Relevant to Health. *Journal of Personality*, 77(6), 1747-1776.

- Walen, H. R., & Lachman, M. E. (2000). Social Support and Strain from Partner, Family, and Friends: Costs and Benefits for Men and Women in Adulthood. *Journal of Social and Personal Relationships*, 17, 5-30.

- How to Tell If Someone Is Lying to You, According to Body Language Experts. (2018,

November 30). Retrieved from
https://time.com/5443204/signs-lying-body-language-experts/

- The Eyes Don't Have It: Lie Detection and Neuro-Linguistic Programming. (2012, July 11). Retrieved from https://journals.plos.org/plosone/article?id=10.1371/journal.pone.0040259

- Maslow's hierarchy of needs. (2002, December 30). Retrieved from https://en.wikipedia.org/wiki/Maslow%27s_hierarchy_of_needs

- Vozza, S. (2017, March 17). 6 Ways To Become A Better Listener. Retrieved from https://www.fastcompany.com/3068959/6-ways-to-become-a-better-listener

- 403 Forbidden. (n.d.). Retrieved from https://www.psychologytoday.com/us/blog/let-their-words-do-the-talking/201106/reading-people-the-words-they-speak

- Leikas, S. (2017, October 1). *Happy Now, Tired Later? Extraverted and Conscientious Behavior Are Related to Immediate Mood Gains, but to Later Fatigue.* Wiley Online Library. https://onlinelibrary.wiley.com/doi/abs/10.1111/jopy.12264